50-90

D0184739

Columbia University

Contributions to Education

Teachers College Series

No. 55

AMS PRESS
NEW YORK

THE PENNSYLVANIA STATE NORMAL SCHOOLS AND PUBLIC SCHOOL SYSTEM

144732

BY

ERNEST O. HOLLAND, Ph. D.

SUPERINTENDENT OF PUBLIC SCHOOLS,
LOUISVILLE, KENTUCKY
SOMETIME FELLOW IN EDUCATION
TEACHERS COLLEGE, COLUMBIA UNIVERSITY

TEACHERS COLLEGE, COLUMBIA UNIVERSITY
CONTRIBUTIONS TO EDUCATION, NO. 55

LB1944
H6
1972

PUBLISHED BY
𝕿𝖊𝖆𝖈𝖍𝖊𝖗𝖘 𝕮𝖔𝖑𝖑𝖊𝖌𝖊, 𝕮𝖔𝖑𝖚𝖒𝖇𝖎𝖆 𝕌𝖓𝖎𝖛𝖊𝖗𝖘𝖎𝖙𝖞
NEW YORK CITY
1912

Library of Congress Cataloging in Publication Data

Holland, Ernest Otto, 1874-1950.
The Pennsylvania State normal schools and public
school system.

Reprint of the 1912 ed., issued in series: Teachers
College, Columbia University. Contributions to education, no. 55.
Originally presented as the author's thesis, Columbia.
1. Teachers' Colleges--Pennsylvania. 2. Public
schools--Pennsylvania. I. Title. II. Series: Columbia University. Teachers College. Contributions to
education, no. 55.
LB1944.H6 1972   370'.73'09748   71-176871
ISBN 0-404-55055-X

Reprinted by Special Arrangement with Teachers
College Press, New York, New York

From the edition of 1912, New York
First AMS edition published in 1972
Manufactured in the United States

AMS PRESS, INC.
NEW YORK, N.Y. 10003

PREFACE

This study in practical school administration was undertaken in the spring of 1910 in connection with the graduate work I was then doing at Teachers College. Grateful acknowledgment for helpful criticisms and suggestions is especially due the committee in charge of my dissertation,—Professors Monroe, Suzzallo and Strayer. I am also indebted to Professor E. L. Thorndike and Mr. M. B. Hillegas, of Teachers College, who carefully examined the statistical tables I have prepared in connection with my study. To Professor E. P. Cubberley, of Leland Stanford, Junior, University, I am indebted for the critical examination of several of the chapters and to Mr. H. B. Moore, of the Boys High School, Louisville, Kentucky, for assistance in revising my manuscript. Finally, I must take this opportunity to thank the leading educators of Pennsylvania for their suggestions and encouragement and for the careful reading of my thesis.

E. O. H.

Louisville, Kentucky, April, 1912.

CONTENTS

THE PENNSYLVANIA STATE NORMAL SCHOOLS AND PUBLIC SCHOOL SYSTEM

CHAPTER I

INTRODUCTION: OBJECT AND SCOPE OF INVESTIGATION

The writer has undertaken to present a critical survey of the provision made in the state of Pennsylvania for the training of teachers in the state normal schools. A study of this kind might be undertaken with regard to any one of several aspects of any state system of education. In any such study the method must be largely comparative. The basis of the criticism which is expressed as the result of such an investigation is, of necessity, that practice found elsewhere in the United States which is commonly considered more satisfactory from the standpoint of our ideals of educational efficiency. We have not yet developed methods of measurement which will enable one to prove either the efficiency or inefficiency of any part of our school system by applying objective measures other than those commonly employed in the comparisons indicated above.

The thirteen state normal schools of Pennsylvania were examined as to management and control, equipment, teaching force, and student body. The school work of these institutions was also carefully examined to discover their influence upon the entire public school system of the state. For this purpose the writer spent in Pennsylvania from the middle of March until the first of June, 1910, visiting these institutions. He went into the classrooms and personally questioned hundreds of students as to their previous academic preparation. He also inspected the general equipment, held conferences with prominent citizens of the locality, with the principals of the normal schools, and with members of the boards of trustees. Finally, by visiting the public schools of the locality, he endeavored to discover how they were affected by the presence of a state normal school. In addition,

I

the writer has been aided in the study by leading educators of the state who have offered many valuable suggestions and have carefully examined and criticised the manuscript.

Soon after the inquiry was begun, the investigator was impressed with the influence exerted by the thirteen normal schools of the state. It seemed to him that these schools, privately controlled and managed, although supported by public funds, are the dominant educational influence of the state. It appeared also that the normal schools of Pennsylvania occupy a dual position: that they were at the same time training schools for teachers and secondary or college preparatory schools. The relation of the normal schools to the whole school system of the state is indicated in the following chart:

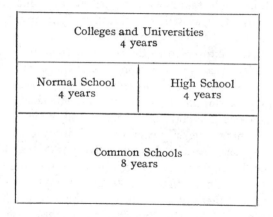

The state of Pennsylvania is appropriating public money both for the public high schools and for the normal schools, which are doing largely the same kind of work. Because of this duplication in function, the academic work in both types of institution is seriously affected; the enrollment in the secondary schools of the state is comparatively small; the proportion of high schools of the lowest grade is abnormally large; and the geographical distribution of all grades of secondary schools has been largely determined by the location of the state normal schools.

Contrasted with the educational status in Pennsylvania, below appears a chart, showing the relationship of the various types of institution, which experience in the most progressive states has demonstrated will produce the best results:

Normal School 2 years	Colleges and Universities 4 years
High School 4 years	
Common Schools 8 years	

The Pennsylvania school code of 1911 is a step in the right direction, but Pennsylvania cannot hope to rank with the best states of the country unless she is willing to go further in constructive school legislation. This new law of 1911 provides for the establishment of a state board of education. Later, when additional laws are enacted giving this central board wide powers in the examination and certification of teachers, in the distribution of public funds to local communities and in the careful supervision of all publicly-supported schools, then Pennsylvania will have in many respects a modern public school system.

It should be noted here, moreover, that the new school code has made provision, enabling the state to acquire possession of the normal schools. This cannot be accomplished for several years, but when it is accomplished, the duplication of work by the normal schools and the high schools will cease, the former devoting themselves to the training of teachers, the latter to the strictly academic preparation of boys and girls to enter the higher institutions of learning—which will then include the normal schools— or directly into the varying activities of life. Of course, the transition will, of necessity, be gradual rather than abrupt. It will be necessary, if the state is to develop a unified system of education, so to arrange the courses in the normal schools that every encouragement will be given to the local community to provide high school education in preparation for professional training in the normal school. To this end full credit in the normal school course as at present organized, should be given for work done in high schools which are recognized by the state department. In order to develop professional training based upon a four years' high school course, the normal schools should offer courses leading to recognition, by diploma or otherwise, in advance of that now commonly offered to students who complete a four year normal school course on the basis of merely elementary school training.

CHAPTER II

HISTORY OF THE ESTABLISHMENT OF THE PENN-SYLVANIA STATE NORMAL SCHOOLS

In order to understand clearly the establishment and the present condition of the Pennsylvania state normal schools, it is necessary to trace the movement which led up to the passage of the normal school act of 1857.

With the exception of Delaware, Tennessee, Alabama, and Florida, all the states of the Union maintain separate normal schools for the training of teachers which receive funds from the public treasury. In Pennsylvania alone these schools are private corporations over which the state exercises little effectual control. In all the other states the normals are an integral part of the state educational system, under the complete control of state authorities. Whether this policy of state subvention, as contrasted with state control, is of itself likely to produce good results should appear from an examination of actual conditions in the thirteen normal schools of this state.

The policy of subvention is, apparently, consistent with the general educational policy. There is no state university. Pennsylvania State College, which receives the money from the Federal land grants, has only three representatives on a governing board of thirty-two members. Moreover, in other fields the same policy prevails. Private hospitals throughout the state receive state aid in large appropriations, unchecked by state direction.

As early as 1749 the leading citizens of Pennsylvania realized that definite steps must be taken to provide well-qualified teachers, and from that year to 1786 many schools were authorized to aid in the preparation of teachers. This work they did on their own initiative until 1786, when, through the efforts of Doctor Benjamin Rush, the state adopted a policy which it continued for fifty years " of chartering colleges and academies and aiding them by appropriations from the public treasury, on the

5

ground, and with the expectation, that in addition to their proper functions they would prepare teachers of lower grade."

Under the authority of the act of 1786 several schools[1] established courses for the training of teachers, and received small sums from the state in recognition. This was the status of teacher-training in Pennsylvania until 1840.

By act of legislature in 1840, the Joliet Academy of Erie county, was recognized as an institution " for the instruction and qualification of teachers of common schools." This institution received no aid from the state; it was erected through local subscription, and for a few years it probably aided considerably in the training of teachers for Erie and Crawford counties. Because of the popular belief at this time that all persons intending to teach should be especially prepared, many academies advertised that they offered courses in education. This was particularly true from 1834 to the passage of the normal school act of 1857 which committed the Commonwealth to a definite policy with respect to the professional preparation of teachers.

In 1854 the office of county superintendent was established by law. As soon as the direction of the common schools of Pennsylvania was given over to those new officers, it became evident that many schools were in very incompetent hands, and the need for well prepared teachers was more keenly felt than ever before. Owing to the fact that the state did not have institutions giving professional work, a local substitute had to be found, and during the first year of the existence of county superintendents, six or eight of the best counties established local and temporary schools for teachers. Their example was followed by other superintendents for the next few years. The largest and most prosperous of these local schools was the " Normal Institute," begun in 1855 at Millersville, Lancaster county, by James P. Wickersham who later became state superintendent. Its success was so great that many of the citizens of Lancaster county contributed money freely in order to erect a permanent county normal school. This institution was looked upon as a model for those the state should establish, since it showed what splendid results could be accomplished in the preparation of teachers.

---

[1] Washington College, Jefferson College, Reading Academy, Pennsylvania College, Allegheny College and Marshall College among the number.

In the meantime, the leading educators began to urge that the state no longer leave entirely to local initiative the important duty of giving normal instruction. They believed that in some way the state should recognize the work that those local normal schools were doing, though it should not support them. This policy was advocated by Burrowes in an article published in 1866 in Barnard's Journal, in which he said: " Normal Schools, like other professional institutions, ought not to be established by and at the expense of the State, and should be no further controlled by the State than is necessary to give value and authority to their diplomas." Other leading educators also advocated this policy which was finally adopted when the normal school act was passed.

In 1856 Thomas H. Burrowes, at the request of State Superintendent Curtin, made a statement outlining the kind of institution that might be approved by the state. This plan, with few modifications, was drafted into a bill which was presented to the Pennsylvania legislature in 1857 and adopted by that body.

The act contained the following provisions:

1. The state to be divided into twelve districts, each with a normal school.

2. These schools to be erected and controlled by private corporations. A corporation might have as few as thirteen contributors or stockholders.

3. Pecuniary affairs to be managed by a board of trustees. No contributor or stockholder to have more than five votes at the election of trustees. No religious test for contributor, stockholder, trustee, professor, or student. A detailed fiscal report to be made out annually to the state superintendent.

4. Following requirements as to equipment:

    a. Ten acres of land.

    b. Buildings for accommodation of three hundred students.

    c. Model school containing at least one hundred students.

    d. Faculty of at least six professors.

5. Course of study and entrance qualifications to be determined by normal school principals when approved by the state superintendent.

6. Each normal school to admit one student annually from each common school district (in the normal school district) at not more than five dollars per term to be paid by the local board

of school directors. Said student to teach in his own district at least three years after graduating.

7. Examinations for graduation to be conducted by a board of principals; certificates or diplomas granted. After two terms of successful teaching each normal school graduate to be given permanent license to teach anywhere in the state. Teachers in service, holding provisional certificates, also to take the examinations in order to receive a higher certificate.

In the main, these were the conditions laid down by law for the establishment and maintenance of normal schools, which were to receive absolutely no financial support from the state. Each institution at the beginning was free to elect any number of trustees and to manage its affairs with practically no interference from the state.

The first school recognized under this act as a state normal school was located at Millersville in Lancaster county. In 1854 the office of county superintendent was established by law. Shortly thereafter the citizens of Millersville were erecting an academy that should carry the pupils somewhat beyond the common school branches. County Superintendent Wickersham, who felt that something must be done to prepare new teachers and improve those already in the service, learned that the academy buildings when completed might serve his purpose in conducting a teachers' school. The trustees not only offered him the use of these buildings, but even offered him one thousand dollars to assist in the conduct of the school. This plan was accepted, and, as has been stated elsewhere, the school was begun as the "Lancaster County Normal Institute" on April 17, 1855, under the direction of the county superintendent.

From the beginning the institution was so prosperous and seemed to meet the needs of the community so well, that the trustees and other leading citizens held several conferences and decided to change its character, giving more attention to the professional preparation of teachers than to the purely cultural work, to enlarge the building to suit the purpose, and finally, to establish a permanent normal school. In the fall of the same year the plans were consummated.

As soon as the act of 1857 was passed, the trustees began to make efforts to meet the requirements. This meant considerable expenditure for equipment, additional land, and a larger faculty.

Great interest was taken,—leading citizens from adjoining counties and even the governor and state superintendent attended a public meeting and urged those who could do so to assist this institution to meet the rather high standards laid down by the act of 1857. All the stipulations were finally met in December, 1859, when the proper authorities recognized the institution as the first so-called state normal school.

From the beginning the Millersville normal school has had a large attendance and has been prosperous. It began with a subscribed stock of $25,000 and a bonded indebtedness of $25,000 additional. There was also a small floating indebtedness. Because of the location of the school and its efficient management, it actually made money and a few thousand dollars were annually added to the sinking fund. It asked for no appropriation from the state and it received none. It was purely a private institution whose work had been approved by the state and whose diplomas were, according to the law, given recognition by the public school officials.

The early history of the next four normal schools to be established is identically parallel with that of Millersville. Private institutions, they exerted themselves to reach the requirements set by the act of 1857, and when those requirements were met, they were recognized as state normals, no one of them having asked or received state aid in any form. Edinboro Normal School, located in Erie county, was recognized in 1861; Mansfield Normal, located at Mansfield, Tioga county, in 1862; Kutztown Normal School, in Berks county, in 1866; Bloomsburg Normal School, at Bloomsburg, Columbia county, in 1869.

In the history of the establishment of the West Chester Normal School in 1871, and the Shippensburg Normal in 1873 there is one significant variation. Toward the purchase of land and the erection of buildings the state gave to the West Chester Normal School the sum of $15,000 and shortly after to the Shippensburg Normal School $35,000, though both remained, equally with the schools previously established, purely private institutions.

The establishment and final recognition of the eighth normal school, located at California, marks a complete change of policy by the state. Up to this time all the institutions had been built entirely through private initiative and support, as the act of 1857 stipulated, though two had been aided by specific appropriations from the state. But the circumstances of the establishment of this school were different.

During the movement for better prepared teachers, few institutions in the southwestern part of the state offered instruction to persons preparing to teach and, as a result, the county superintendents were compelled to conduct temporary normal institutes; but finally in 1862 a building was erected at Millsboro, Washington county, and a permanent normal school established. However, the school met with some discouragements and two of the teachers accepted positions in the academy located at California. This academy had been in existence since 1852, and in 1859 an attempt was made to induce the legislature to lower the standards set by the normal school act and accept the academy with its poorer equipment. The legislature did pass an act to this effect, but the governor wisely vetoed it.

In 1865, the legislature was induced to grant a charter to the " South Western Normal College," which name should continue " until and before the time when it may be recognized as a State Normal School." The citizens of the town refused to give more money to this new venture unless the state would pledge itself to accept the institution when the improvements were completed. Therefore, in 1869 the legislature was asked to enter into a contract binding the state to accept the institution after certain conditions were complied with. This act stipulated that the state superintendent's approval of the town of California as a suitable location for a state normal school was to be the first step. Then, if the president of the board of trustees of the South Western Normal School would state under oath " that said College has a bona fide subscription fund for the erection of its buildings, a sum of at least twenty thousand dollars, and that there is expended in the erection of their buildings a sum of at least ten thousand," then the state would aid to the extent of five thousand dollars. And in the next two years, if the college authorities expended thirty thousand dollars, the state promised to give the ten thousand dollars.

As early as 1872, the friends of the California institution were able to get the additional grant of $10,000 though it was not recognized by the state until 1874. The other existing normal schools were practically under the control of private individuals, —the stockholders—and in no true sense could they be called state institutions; but the men interested in the California Normal School were able to change the attitude of the legislature toward state adoption and state support, though still leaving the control in the hands of private individuals.

Since 1874 the policy of the state has followed the precedent set in the case of the California Normal. Five additional state normals have been recognized, and in each instance the state has assisted with increasingly liberal appropriations, at the same time leaving the schools under private management and control. The schools so established are: Indiana Normal, in Indiana county, recognized in 1875; Lock Haven in Clinton county, in 1877; Clarion Normal, in Clarion county, in 1886; Slippery Rock, in Butler county, in 1889; and the last of Pennsylvania's state normals at East Stroudsburg, in Monroe county, in 1893.

This brief history of the establishment of the thirteen state normal schools shows how the spirit of the original act of 1857 was misinterpreted or consciously modified. The legislature which passed this act did not hold out a promise of any kind and did not offer financial assistance under any circumstances. When gradually the state was induced to give special grants for the establishment of these schools and later to make annual appropriations for their maintenance, these institutions became what they are today,—publicly-supported institutions under the control and ownership of private corporations.

CHAPTER III

PRESENT MANAGEMENT

For many years, the national and many of the state governments have required the officials in charge of public institutions to render a full and strict accounting of their stewardship. These detailed reports are always open to the public: any taxpayer may go to one of these institutions and personally examine the records and books. Public control has extended even to private business: within the past few years the national and most of the state governments have passed stringent laws regulating the conduct of corporations, both large and small, and of insurance and railroad companies. In fact, all private institutions that affect to any extent the public welfare have been placed under public supervision and control. In the light of these facts, it is startling to find in the wealthy and populous state of Pennsylvania institutions that are publicly supported but privately controlled, that render only stereotyped reports and that are practically free from state supervision. Probably in no other state of the Union can a like condition be found.

As has been explained previously, the so-called state normal schools have been, and are, conducted as private corporations with practically no control on the part of the state. The law of 1857 simply stipulated that there should be not less than 13 contributors or stockholders, and "that the pecuniary affairs of each of said schools shall be managed, and the general control exercised by a Board of Trustees, (whose officers shall be a President and Secretary who shall, and a Treasurer who shall not, be members of said Board,) to be chosen by the contributors or stockholders on the first Monday in May annually; but no contributor, or stockholder shall have more than five votes at the election of trustees. . . ."

The state could take no direct part in the election of trustees, since, under the law, these schools were private institutions; but as soon as the state began to give them money, many legislators

12

and educators contended that it should have something to say as to how these appropriations should be spent. Therefore in February, 1872, the legislature passed an act providing that no board should have more than 15 members, and authorizing the State Superintendent "to appoint two citizens to act as trustees" of each normal school "on the part of the State." In April of the same year it further stipulated that no school " shall receive an appropriation from the State" unless these two persons appointed by the State Superintendent were permitted "to act as trustees on the part of the state, with all the rights and privileges of other trustees."

In 1875, the State passed an act requiring each state normal school to "be managed by a board of eighteen trustees, twelve elected by the contributors or stockholders and six appointed by the Superintendent of Public Instruction." In 1907, the latter number was increased to nine. These nine were to be appointed by the State Superintendent from a list of twice that number, submitted to him by the stockholders. However, if these nominees should not be satisfactory to him, "he shall, with the advice and consent of the governor, choose others deemed more suitable." But in spite of these provisions, owing to the natural difficulty experienced by the State Superintendent to discover incompetence, the evils of the private corporation still persist.

Seldom does the State Superintendent interfere by refusing to appoint those nominated by the stockholders. Recently, the present incumbent has made a ruling to the effect that he would not appoint as trustee to represent the state anyone who is a stockholder in the normal school corporation. But at a moment's notice a stockholder can transfer his holdings to his wife, to his five-year-old son, or to an accommodating neighbor, and then the man is eligible to become a state trustee. In some respects this ruling does harm for it encourages duplicity. Often a man owning stock is much more conscientious and careful in guarding the interests of the state than is a bank clerk, or book-keeper, who is employed by a stockholder and a trustee and who as a "dummy" votes as he is told. The ruling of the state superintendent will not in any sense meet the difficulty.

In practically all the so-called State Normal Schools of Pennsylvania—schools conducted as private corporations—the stock has been gradually purchased by a very small group of men, who absolutely control the institutions which receive hundreds of thousands of dollars annually from the state. Many kinds of organizations are found: in one place a bank controls; in another three or four men, including a banker, dominate the close corporation; in still another, one man who owns a majority of the stock and who selects his own board of trustees, is principal of the institution and receives a large salary; in another, two or three men connected with the institution hold a majority of the stock, have themselves elected to positions in the school and determine their own salaries. Strange as it may seem, in many cases the men who dominate did not contribute any considerable amount to the erection or growth of the institution they manage. In one or two instances, the control has been purchased for two or three hundred dollars, though in others, as much as eight or ten thousand has been given by one or two men to obtain practical ownership of property which, to-day, because of the sacrifice of others and the bounty of the state, is worth from two hundred thousand to three-quarters of a million dollars.

The Millersville State Normal School. Recognized by the State in 1859.

At the Millersville State Normal School, the oldest of the thirteen institutions, one man, the principal, holds a majority of the stock, and so is the practical owner of a plant worth over a half-million dollars. Of this amount the state has contributed over $380,000.[1]

The story of the handling of stock at Millersville goes back to the very beginning. This normal school started with a subscribed stock of $25,000, widely scattered among the leading citizens of Millersville and Lancaster county. The par value of the shares was $25. There was also a bonded indebtedness of $25,000 additional, with a small floating indebtedness. At

---

[1] The following statements concerning the management and condition of the Pennsylvania state normal schools are based upon a personal investigation made by the author during the spring and summer of 1910. The author is not conversant with changes that may have been made since that date.

the beginning this institution asked for no aid from the state, and it would have been successful for a good many years, probably, without any help. Later, however, it received a good deal of money from the state. By 1878 the amount of money given by Pennsylvania as a direct gift, had exceeded $55,000 and the appropriations to graduates were in excess of $3,000. During this year, the trustees passed a resolution to the effect that any stockholder might dispose of his holdings to the institution at their face value, or he might contribute the stock if he preferred. This action was taken by the trustees for the ostensible purpose of doing away with the stock control and preventing attempts to declare dividends.

But there is another phase of the story that must not be omitted. For a number of years previous to this action of the board a few of the trustees quietly bought up or had given to them large blocks of stock. This was not a difficult thing to do, since the shares were considered practically worthless. Upon good authority, it was learned that three trustees cleared up among them the sum of $15,000. All told a little over $22,000 was spent in buying up the normal school stock. About eighty-five per cent of the shares were purchased at par, with an additional four per cent given outright by public-spirited citizens who refused to turn a philanthropic venture into profit. About ten per cent of the stock was still held by the trustees of the normal school. These shares, less than two hundred in number, were surrendered by these officials, who received in their place "certificates of contribution," which carried with them the same privileges as the original shares of stock so that each holder of a certificate might vote for the trustees. Since the stockholders had surrendered their rights, the owners of the certificates became the permanent managers of the school with no possibility of having the control wrested from them. In a word, these men had acquired absolute control, and this control was gained at a cash profit of from fifteen to twenty thousand dollars.

When the stock was transferred into "certificates of contribution," the control of the institution fell into the hands of three or four men. The complete domination of the few men who owned the certificates of contribution continued for twenty-five years. In 1903 or 1904, a man living at Lancaster, four miles away, began to buy up all the certificates he could. It is estimated that he was compelled to pay from two to four times their par value because their purchase meant the permanent control of an institution whose yearly income was over $100,000. In the spring of 1904, the principal bought a controlling interest in the normal school, and to-day he probably holds all but seventy-five or eighty of the hundred and eighty-nine certificates of contribution.

In a good many respects the institution at present is in better hands than it has been in the twenty-five years preceding the purchase of the certificates by the principal; but this condition is no argument for the situation as it stands to-day. Here is an institution liberally supported by the state and controlled by one man who may dismiss half his teachers at a moment's notice, or reconstruct his board of trustees. The members of the board, instead of having to look to a large body of stockholders in the community or to the state as a whole for approval of their acts, have simply to turn to one man, the principal: if he approves, they continue in office; if he objects, half the members of the board, (those representing " the contributors ") will not receive his support for re-election when their term expires, and the other half, (those representing the state) will not be recommended by him to the state superintendent for reappointment. This means that in time he can rid himself of any trustee that objects to him personally or to his methods of conducting the school.

Date of visit: March 24 and May 18 and 19, 1910.

The Edinboro State Normal School. Recognized by the state in 1861.

In 1861 when the Edinboro Academy was transformed into the present institution, which was accepted by the state as a normal school, several hundred shares were issued, representing donations by private citizens of amounts varying from five dollars to one thousand dollars each. A gift, regardless of its size, meant a vote. In this school there has been a long struggle for control, and there has also been the same speculation with stock as at Millersville, though not with the intention of selling it to the institution or to the state. Nearly from the beginning there has been trouble, either between the principal and his trustees, or between the management and the town. In 1892, the fight happened to be between the principal, J. A. Cooper, and a majority of his board. After these men had employed detective methods against the head of the school, they called a special meeting of the board and dismissed him. Practically the entire student body and nearly all the teachers rallied to his support. As a consequence, a large number of the students entered another normal school, and the institution dwindled from over six hundred to fifteen students, " consisting largely of the children of the trustees and their immediate friends."

For a long time, possibly for twenty-five years, a small group of men has dominated this school, and the contest for the past two elections, which involved the entire village, has mainly been to unseat these men. As a consequence, the model school has gradually dwindled until it has less than ninety pupils in all the grades; and several of the classes number less than five pupils. The practice teaching is therefore really worthless.

Evidence of the domination of this group is the fact that its members furnished practically all the supplies to the normal school. Especially was this true before the law of April 23, 1903, which made it a misdemeanor for a trustee to furnish supplies to a normal school, but even after the passage of this act some of the trustees were willing to take their chances with the enforcement of the law.[1]

In the spring of 1909 State Superintendent Schaeffer learned of the election contest, and finally he and the governor appointed two or three non-partisans. Shortly after these men came on the board, expert auditors were employed to go over the books of the school corporation. There seems to be conclusive evidence that the system of bookkeeping was miserable and that for several years no method was employed to keep a complete record of expenditures and receipts.

Since the members appointed in May, 1909, by the governor and the state superintendent have been on the board, the whole system of bookkeeping has been reconstructed, many of the abuses have disappeared and the entire school will probably be put upon a better financial and educational plane.

Date of visit: April 15, 16, 17, 18 and 19, 1910.

---

[1] The writer examined the secretary's books and records from 1900 to 1910.

The Mansfield State Normal School. Recognized by the state in 1862.

The history of the Mansfield Normal School is similar to that of both Millersville and Edinboro. When the school became a so-called state institution in 1864, the 375 shares of stock were widely distributed. Some of these had been paid in cash—fifty dollars a share—by the business men in the village and the well-to-do farmers of Tioga county; and some of the shares were given to persons who had made their contribution to the educational institution through work on the buildings or grounds. When the school began to send out well-prepared teachers to Tioga and adjoining counties, the people were glad that they had assisted in its creation and growth. Gradually, however, tho$^\mathrm{se}$ farmers living some distance from the village neglected or were unable to attend the annual meeting of the stockholders; others that had given freely to the institution moved away. Later, when the older donors died, the stock fell into the hands of younger persons who looked upon it as a doubtful asset, regarding it as an empty heritage rather than a real obligation. Finally, only those in the village of Mansfield were sufficiently in touch with the work and the needs of the school to attend the elections and become members of the board of trustees. The individuals especially interested were those who furnished supplies to the school or who had sons or daughters in attendance.

One of the citizens of Mansfield, Mr. Charles Ross, the banker, began to see the possibilities of owning a controlling interest in the school. For several years Mr. Ross had bought normal school stock and had urged his friends to follow his example. To-day he personally owns as much as sixty-five or seventy-five shares. For some of this stock he probably paid but $5.00; some of it may have been given him; but after the contest between the Ross party and the other side became heated, stock sold for $50.00. Since the law permits an individual to vote but five shares, the banker has distributed his additional holdings in blocks of five among his friends and employes. At the annual election, Mr. Ross obtains proxies from these persons, or he induces them to attend the contest and vote his ticket.

Last year the Ross faction won the contest, elected three men, and nominated six other partisans to State Superintendent

Schaeffer, who, after investigating the situation, appointed three non-partisans living outside the village. These men prevented Mr. Ross and his adherents from dismissing the principal and two or three other teachers. But in the meantime, Mr. Ross has purchased more stock, and to-day he and a small group of his friends absolutely control the institution. If Superintendent Schaeffer again appoints three unbiased men to represent the state, the condition of the school may not be impaired by the dismissal of men who have conducted the school in an efficient manner; but there is great danger either that these teachers will refuse to remain longer under such adverse conditions, or that Mr. Ross may win over to his side one of the state's representatives, and then the school may be disrupted.

Date of visit: April 5 and 6, 1910.

The Kutztown State Normal School. Recognized by the state in 1866.

In 1866 the Kutztown Normal School was given state recognition. At that time 240 shares were issued on donations of $24,000 for land and buildings. This institution was established by the Germans of Berks county to furnish better educational advantages for their children. Here as elsewhere there has been a gradual concentration of the active stock, and the control now rests very largely in the hands of two or three families.

One German family controls forty-six shares of stock. Each member of this family having more than five shares has distributed them so that the full voting power can be utilized in an emergency. At the annual election held in May, 1910, but twenty-nine votes were cast, so it would seem that no one except those directly connected with the school, either as employe or as trustee, attends these important meetings. The purpose of the founders and of the state has been defeated since the stockholding feature of these schools was to arouse the intelligent interest of an entire community.

Date of visit: May 5, 1910.

The Bloomsburg Literary Institute and State Normal School. Recognized by the state in 1869.

The Bloomsburg Normal School, from 1869, when it was accepted, till 1890 or later, was in such financial difficulties that it attracted the attention only of men who were genuinely interested in the school. Gradually, however, the financial side became better and as this occurred, the active stock found its way into the hands of a few men. To-day the school plant is estimated to be worth over $600,000; the funds of the school are kept in one bank, and something very similar to a close corporation exists. Most of the heavy stockholders are trustees and they take considerable pride in the institution which they direct. The stock has no particular value and there has been but one important contest in recent years in the selection of members of the board. Proof that the stock of the Bloomsburg Normal School is owned or controlled by a small group of men is found in the annual election of trustees by the stockholders at the May meeting this year (1910). Between four and five hundred shares were represented, but not over fifteen men were in attendance. In this school, contrary to the spirit of the law, practically every state trustee owns stock. In fact, of the nine men who were chosen to guard the State's interests, all but one either own outright or control a number of shares.

Date of visit: March 31 and May 28, 1910.

The West Chester State Normal School. Recognized by the state in 1871.

From the beginning, up to nearly the present day, the West Chester Normal School has been fairly well managed. Its control rested with the owners of the 825 shares of stock, which were sold originally at fifty dollars a share. These shares were widely distributed for a long time, for every public-spirited citizen, who was financially able, had been called upon to assist in the making of a state normal. Even during the first year, 1871, it was necessary for the state to assist to the extent of fifteen thousand dollars.

For a long time this stock was considered worthless, but later, when the attendance increased and the state gave more freely, this stock began to be very valuable from one point of view: each of the West Chester banks wanted to keep the normal school deposits and to transact its business. Finally, several years ago, directors of a prominent national bank spent several thousand dollars for normal school stock. They turned into the collateral security fund of their national bank all of this stock for which they had paid from six to fifteen dollars a share, and it seemed that their action had neither cost them anything nor harmed the bank. Later, however, the national bank examiner or the government comptroller objected to this arrangement and the result was that either the bank or these men had to replace the money which they had spent for normal school stock. After considerable discussion among the bank directors, two of them stood personally responsible for the cost of this stock and so became the practical owners of the institution worth over a half million dollars, toward the management and development of which the State had already given over $300,000.

In 1908 after several consultations among the three or four men holding a majority of stock, these men requested in writing the president of the board, Levi G. McCauley, to call a special meeting of the trustees. This meeting was held December 7, 1908, and resolutions were offered that the West Chester Normal School " purchase . . . . such of its capital stock, not however to exceed 800 shares thereof, ... and pay for each share thereof the sum of $50.00, the par value . . . .," and that " the said school shall borrow the moneys needed for the purchase thereof . . . ." The eighteen members of the board attended this meeting and the vote on the resolutions carried by twelve for and six against.

A number of the stockholders in the West Chester Normal School, including two or three trustees, brought suit against the president, secretary, and treasurer of the school, and asked for an injunction to prevent the buying of the stock. Because of a technical legal mistake in the wording of the resolutions submitted to the trustees at the meeting on December 7, another meeting was called on December 31, 1908, and this fault was rectified. In the end, the court ruled that the action taken by a majority of the board of trustees was legal, and at once the injunction was dissolved. Since then, stock offered for sale has been purchased by the school.

In order to show the spirit of these men who practically own the West Chester Normal School, one should read the answer of the defendants to the request of the plaintiffs in the injunction suit brought by the latter. Paragraph ten of the request states that "the only income of said corporation the Normal School is derived from the tuition and board of students, and from appropriations made by the State of Pennsylvania . . . . and said State further contributes aid to students thereat desiring education; that its revenues from all sources are no more than sufficient to meet legitimate operating expenses from year to year, and to make the necessary extensions and improvements to carry out the objects of its incorporation." The reply to this was that the school made money and that very recently as much as $60,000 had been spent on unnecessary extensions and improvements. "The unnecessary expense" referred to was for a new library with modern equipment.

In another paragraph, the defendants object to the salaries paid the teachers; they believe that these salaries are very high. The average salary paid the men teachers at West Chester, exclusive of the principal's salary, is $1,541.66, and that paid the women is $812.50.

In paragraph fourteen, of the answers of the defendants, we come upon this statement: "The tangible property and assets of the corporation are worth, as we believe, $750,000 or more; the indebtedness of the corporation, according to the plaintiffs' averment, is but $142,800, so that over and above all indebtedness there is actual and tangible property to the amount of $600,000, or thereabouts. *This property belongs to the shareholders, owning 825 shares of the capital stock, so that each share thereof, is worth in the neighborhood of $700, instead of $50.*" These statements were made regardless of the fact that the state had given the normal school between three and four hundred thousand dollars.

Date of visit: May 13, 14, 16, and 17, 1910.

The Shippensburg State Normal School. Recognized by the state in 1873.

The Shippensburg Normal School is controlled by a small group of men whom it would be practically impossible to dispossess. Several years ago George H. Stewart, a wealthy banker and a dominant figure in the affairs of the town, became interested in the conduct of the normal school. When the institution was started in 1871, he was a contributor, and later he probably was called upon to assist it over financial difficulties. In recent years, the school has been rather prosperous, and its complete control is now in the hands of Mr. Stewart, his bank (the First National), and his immediate friends.

It has been stated above that the group of men now controlling this school were not in any danger of having to surrender to another group. There is one definite reason for this assertion: the stock book is so complicated and so unintelligible that no one can state exactly how much stock is outstanding. At the beginning, probably 800 shares were issued at $25 a share. Of these, the late Captain T. P. Blair, who donated the land for the school, received half, which he scattered very widely for voting purposes. Some of these shares have been lost and others have been given to or purchased by the bank group at little cost.

About 1895, the trustees voted that one-third of the tuition might be paid by normal stock. Only sons and daughters of stockholders were supposed to receive such reductions, but it was an exceedingly easy matter for a parent to purchase the necessary stock and thereby get the reduced tuition. Later, an enterprising boarding-house keeper bought up a good many shares at a low figure and offered to furnish stock free of charge to all pupils that would board with him. The trustees at once rescinded their former action, and since then no stock has been used to pay tuition either in whole or part.

The normal school has in its possession today ninety shares that have been cancelled; other shares were partly exhausted before the board reversed its former ruling, and it is very hard to say who owns voting-stock and who does not. Undoubtedly, however, the bank group has enough shares to prevent any outsider from disturbing it. At the recent election in May, 1910, but five persons attended, and seventy votes were cast. Two of these are officers of the First National and one of the remainder is the treasurer of the school. Although conditions at Shippensburg do not appear to be bad it is of course evident that a close corporation cannot conduct a school for the best educational interests of the state.

Date of visit: April 8 and July 15, 1910.

The California State Normal School. Recognized by the state in 1874.

For a good many years a small group of men has controlled the California Normal School and this group is in control to-day. When contributions and subscriptions were taken forty years ago, several years before the school was given State recognition, $18,000 was raised, and proportionate stock was issued at $25.00 per share; but at present as far as can be ascertained there are only 560 shares that can be accounted for.

During the thirty-six years of the school's existence, the stock has changed hands rather frequently. At one time, when the institution was less prosperous, the stock was practically worthless, and it was to be had for the asking. Generally, however, it has sold for from $2.50 to $6.00 a share. The banks of the town became interested in the school just as soon as surplus funds had to be cared for, and the stockholders and officers of one of these banks have a great deal to say as to who shall be members of the board of trustees. Some time ago at a meeting of the stockholders the following by-law relating to the matter of counting shares and stock, was passed:

1, 2 or 3 shares equal 1 vote.
4, 5, 6 or 7 shares equal 2 votes.
8, 9, 10 or 11 shares equal 3 votes.
12, 13, 14, or 15 shares equal 4 votes.
16 or more shares equal 5 votes.

This is a very innocent looking rule, but it has actually resulted in preventing the opposition from obtaining control. The average disinterested person, holding sixteen shares for instance, might attend the annual election of trustees in May and cast five votes, or again he might forget the meeting altogether and then his stock would not be voted. Another person, holding sixteen shares of stock and interested in keeping his own position as teacher or officer in the school could, if he chose, bestir himself, go to his relatives and friends, sign over to each of them one share of stock, and, on election day, instead of casting but five, he would be able to cast sixteen votes. In 1909 and in 1910 there have been contested elections in the California normal school, but those in control have not been disturbed. The stock book is in their hands. Whenever they detect activity among the members of the opposition, they have simply to turn to the stock book, make an estimate of how many votes at most can be mustered against them by the widest distribution of shares, and then set to work to distribute their holdings to offset this.

Three persons, who are directly connected with the administration, are able to control 129 votes of the 250 or 300 usually cast at any election, and the present trustees and their immediate friends can furnish enough more votes to save the day. Proof of this statement is to be found in the recent contested election, held May, 1910: of the 350 votes cast, those in power were able to control two hundred. Most of this additional strength came directly from the trustees, for excluding the thirty-seven votes of one person, both a teacher and a trustee, the other trustees were able to cast over seventy, which, added to the one hundred and twenty-nine already accounted for, gave those in control a voting strength of approximately two hundred out of the three hundred and fifty votes.

It must not be inferred that if the opposition took control of the California Normal School the situation would be materially improved; it would simply mean that another close corporation would be formed, which would dominate as it pleased. All those now connected with the school, who own stock, could be dismissed regardless of their efficiency or inefficiency and friends of the opposition chosen to take their places with scant consideration for the welfare of the school and the work it is supposed to do.

Date of visit: April 29 and 30, 1910.

The Indiana State Normal School. Recognized by the state in 1875.

The situation in the Indiana State Normal School is rather unique: the 2080 shares of stock, issued to the donors of the $25,000 for the first school building, are still rather widely distributed, though there are enough shares in the hands of two or three families to control any election. At present, however, these families have not worked together and the ordinary normal school group is not greatly in evidence, though seldom do more than fifteen or twenty persons attend the election of trustees. Yet, it is very possible that some enterprising individual,—a banker or a man desirous of a school position,—

may appear at any time and, with an expenditure of two thousand dollars or less, obtain possession of a plant that has cost the State over $415,000 in direct and special appropriations, and receives between $40,000 and $50,000 more from the State annually. At present the stock sells for only $2.50 a share or ten per cent of its par value.

Though the original normal school act stipulates that no one shall cast more than five votes, the large stockholders at Indiana cast as many votes as they have shares, and one of the trustees claims that the charter granted by the state legislature makes the Indiana normal school corporation an exception and permits what in other schools would be a violation of the law. But even if this were a definite violation, it would not be important since at the other institutions the spirit of the law is evaded by the extensive use of proxies.

The size of the town in which this normal school is located has been in its favor since the local jealousies are never so much in evidence in a city of 10,000 inhabitants as they are in a village or town of one thousand. Besides, there has been little inclination among the trustees of the Indiana normal school to employ home talent regardless of its efficiency. This policy has enabled the school to obtain the services of many promising young men and women from the best American colleges and universities.

Date of visit: April 25, 26, 27, and 28, 1910.

The Lock Haven State Normal School. Recognized by the state in 1877.

The Lock Haven Normal School which was accepted by the State in 1877, was erected through the financial assistance of the State legislature and the subscription by the public-spirited citizens of the county of 869 shares of stock at twenty-five dollars a share.

Up to the present time there has been no demand for the normal school stock. Few shares have changed hands except through death and inheritance. On May 6, 1910, an election of trustees occurred. Thirty-two persons were present, though there was no contest. At this election only sixty-four votes were cast. This small number does not in any sense indicate the number of shares represented, for about twenty years ago, for some reason, a by-law was passed stipulating how the shares should be counted for voting purposes. There has been no disposition to modify this rule, which is as follows:

All persons holding less than 4 shares have 1 vote.

All persons holding 4 and less than 10 shares have 2 votes.

All persons holding 10 and less than 20 shares have 3 votes.

All persons holding 20 and less than 25 shares have 4 votes.

All persons holding 25 and over have 5 votes.

Probably only three men hold in this school corporation as many as forty shares each, and only six or eight others own as many as twenty or thirty shares apiece. The board of trustees seems to be representative, and the citizens generally are interested in the progress of the school. This happy condition is however an accident. The same opportunity for a selfish man or a selfish group to get control exists here as in other similar institutions. Although in this and in one or two other schools, private control for private gain is not a fact, yet it is a danger and under the present system must remain a constant danger.

Date of visit: April 7 and May 28, 1910.

The Clarion State Normal School. Recognized by the state in 1887.

The group method of control came hard upon the heels of the creation of the Clarion State Normal School. Shortly after the school was opened, three or four men took control, and this condition continued until about 1901, when a rupture occurred among the members of the close corporation resulting in the dismissal of the principal. This they were easily able to do by getting into their hands additional normal school stock, and making changes on the board of trustees. In itself this action was not exceptional, for such summary dismissals have occurred in other normal schools of the state; but this particular conflict led to a revelation of conditions that shows still another danger connected with publicly-supported and privately-controlled institutions, for it must be remembered that what has happened at Clarion may happen at any other Pennsylvania normal school.

In 1901, it is stated that Representative John A. F. Hoy, of Clarion County, announced to his friends on the normal school board of trustees that the school could get $40,000 if they bestirred themselves. They followed his suggestion and sent a committee to Harrisburg to ask the legislature to give them that amount for a chapel building. The bill passed the house with little or no opposition, but it is claimed that one of the politicians of the State, James Mitchell, came to Mr. Hoy and the normal school committee and stated that certain members of the Senate intended to offer opposition to this appropriation. Finally this same politician informed them, according to the version given to the public by the deposed principal, that if they would pay him ten per cent of the appropriation, he would manage it. They agreed and the Senate passed the appropriation, but the Governor later reduced it to $27,500.

Shortly after, the two men who owned a majority of the stock submitted Mr. Hoy's name to the Superintendent of Public Instruction as a State trustee, and Mr. Hoy was appointed. Later Mr. James Mitchell went to Clarion presumably to get his percentage of the State's money. Because all normal school expenditures had to be reported under oath to the Auditor General of the State and be approved by him, the trustees began to look about for a method of concealing this transaction. Finally the business manager at that time, who with the registrar was proprietor of the school, said that he had a lot of old pipe in the basement of one of the building which had been there a long time and was worth nothing. He proposed to make out a bill for $2,750, ostensibly for this old scrap and with this money to pay Mr. Mitchell. This was done on August 9, 1901. The nine trustees present voted for the bogus sale. On March 22, 1902, an order was made out in favor of Mr. Hoy who received $2,750 from the school treasury. Mr. Mitchell, the man who had piloted the normal school bill through the Senate, was in Clarion that day, waiting at the hotel; but later he claimed he did not get a penny, while Hoy insisted that the gentleman received the full amount he had demanded and they had promised.

This entire scandal came out because of the anger of Davis, the former principal, due to his dismissal. For some time the Clarion Normal School management was considerably worried, but after months of anxiety, the entire matter was finally dropped. On February 26, 1903, the local paper contained a statement to the effect that Mr. Davis, the former principal, had dismissed his attorneys and had abandoned the prosecution.

As late as July 10, 1903, I. M. Shannon, a prominent banker of the town, published in the local papers a letter to the normal school trustees, which began as follows:

" At a meeting of the board of trustees . . . . on August 9, 1901, there was presented for approval by the registrar, James Pinks,. a certain bill of R. G. Yingling for repairs, etc., amounting to $2,750, which on motion of W. Day Wilson, was approved and the president and secretary were authorized to issue an order for the same; that subsequently to the meeting of the aforesaid, an order was duly issued by the president and the secretary to the said R. G. Yingling, for the said sum of $2,750 for repairs, etc., and on which order J. A. F. Hoy drew said sum of $2,750 out of the treasury of the said school along about the last day of May following. . . .

" Your informant being then and now a stockholder in the said institution, owning two shares of stock . . . . and showing by the statement of facts aforesaid that the said trustees and others have unlawfully taken from the treasury of the said institution the sum of $2,750 of the moneys belonging to the Clarion State Normal School and have never repaid the same, respectfully requests your honorable board to bring a proper action or actions against the parties implicated in the above transaction to the end that the said sum of $2,750 may be restored to the said treasury."

Mr. Shannon, the author of the above letter, is still caring for the normal school funds.

One of the most significant things that came out during the controversy and futile prosecution was a statement by James Pinks, the registrar, who presented the bill rendered by Mr. Yingling for $2,750 for some old iron. Mr. Pinks said:

" The Clarion Normal School is no better nor no worse than twelve other normal schools in this state. They have all paid to get appropriations and I suppose they will all do it again."

Another significant thing is to be found in the fact that there has been no change in the control of the school. Five of the nine men who voted to pay $2,750 for a pile of old iron are still members of the board of trustees.

Recently, the Clarion board of trustees has elected a new man as principal; the work of the institution, from an educational point of view, has improved, and the prospects are good. It is unfortunate, however, that the men who were implicated in the Hoy-Mitchell scandal do not withdraw, but it is practically impossible to depose them, since in addition to the fact that they control a majority of the stock and are able to select half the board outright, their nominations to the state for the other board members are generally accepted. The only way the state can get control is either by buying up the normal stock at par and thereby rewarding these men, or by refusing to aid further a so-called state institution which in the main has been managed by private individuals for their advantage.

Date of visit: April 22 and 23, 1910.

The Slippery Rock State Normal School. Recognized by the state in 1889.

The conditions under which the Slippery Rock Normal School is conducted are not dissimilar from those at California, though the former institution is more prosperous and in it the group domination is more evident and powerful. Twenty years ago the citizens of Slippery Rock and the adjacent country contributed about $20,000 in cash and $15,000 in land donations and labor. Two hundred shares were issued, which were held by about the same number of persons. Because of the location of the town,—four miles from a railroad,—the concerted action on the part of the people to establish an institution of higher learning and to meet the requirements of the normal school act was in itself commendable. Those that had much money gave freely; those that were less able contributed but twenty-five or fifty dollars; and those that could give no money, gladly gave their labor for a few weeks. Practically every one living in or near the little village of Slippery Rock had done something to help establish the normal school. A full share was given for a hundred dollars in cash, land, or labor, but half or quarter shares were also issued. A building was erected in 1889 and in the same year the institution was officially recognized as a state normal school.

At that time the normal school stock was widely distributed, but the school was too prosperous for this condition to continue long. In the past few years the stock has been bought up by a small group. The men belonging to this organization have given from fifteen to one hundred dollars a share in the attempt to obtain absolute control, for though the stock has never paid any dividends, it is a profitable investment in a great many ways. No stock sells below par today and some of it could not be purchased for three or four times its face value. The people who have made these investments are not sentimentalists; they have good business sense. It actually pays to hold the stock, as will be explained later.

This close corporation is a family-faculty-bank affair. Five or six families belong to it with enough votes to elect themselves and their friends to positions on the normal school board of trustees, as directors of the bank, and to positions on the faculty of the school. The Citizens' National Bank keeps the normal school funds, and its president is also president of the normal school board and its cashier is treasurer of the board of trustees. The principal of the normal school and one of the teachers are directors in the same bank, seven of the teachers own stock in the bank, and several others own normal school stock.

There are several good instructors at Slippery Rock, but apparently the question of efficiency is not the only or even the first standard that is laid down. Teachers either belong to prominent families of the community or they and their friends are stockholders. They have become a part of the community life, and it is practically impossible to remove them. An attempt was made several years ago to dismiss two of the teachers, who were said to be unsuccessful in the class-room, but they are still in the school.

Date of visit: April 20 and 21, 1910.

The East Stroudsburg State Normal School. Recognized by the state in 1893.

The last of the thirteen so-called state normal schools was established at East Stroudsburg in 1891 and 1892 and received official recognition in 1893. From nearly the first, this school has had trouble. It is necessary to give some historical details in order to discuss the conditions as they exist today.

The state was deceived in the method of obtaining subscriptions. When the promoters asked for subscriptions, they discovered that the ordinary appeals were hardly sufficient. Finally they hit upon a new device to induce the farmers of the county and the townspeople to subscribe for stock. Anyone taking a block of five shares, for which he paid $500, was to have a scholarship, which would give tuition practically free to one pupil for five years or to five pupils for one year. At that time the state normal schools charged from fifty to sixty dollars for tuition, so this in the end would mean that those having children to educate would be giving to the school only $250.

When those interested in getting the state to adopt this new institution went before the legislature, they stated that $31,750 had been raised. This was very probably the truth, but there had been sold fifty-three blocks of five shares each, which meant in the end that the institution, or rather the state, would be compelled to give back to the subscribers 263 free tuitions at fifty dollars each. This latter amount, $13,250, subtracted from the $31,750, would leave unincumbered only $18,500. This, it is asserted, was not known by the legislature which accepted the school.

Soon after the school was started these scholarships began to assume definite value. Those who had purchased five shares of normal school stock and did not have children to educate began to sell these fifty-dollar scholarships for thirty or forty dollars, though in every other respect the normal school stock was worthless. Several years before, when subscriptions were being taken, the Lackawanna railroad subscribed for $2,000 of stock. As soon as the institution was established, a keen business man is said to have paid the railroad $1,000 for its shares. At a meeting of the board of trustees on November 7, 1898, five years after the state accepted the school, the board ordered that the scholarships be redeemed by the school at the rate now being paid by the school, viz.: $50 for each scholarship. At once this redemption began, and within a year, $4,000 in cash was paid to redeem scholarships.

In the spring of 1905, certain citizens of East Stroudsburg demanded that an investigation be made of the management of the normal school. Attorney Robert K. Young, of Wellsboro, was appointed by Auditor General William P. Snyder to represent the State and make an investigation. He went to East

Stroudsburg and after spending considerable time in his examination reported as follows:

1. Certain members of the board have sold supplies to the school in violation of the law of April 23, 1903.

2. There has been jobbery in the scholarships.

3. The trustees have paid themselves three dollars for attending each session of the board. Their expenses have also been paid. Both of these are clearly against the law.[3]

4. When the school was accepted by the State, false statements were made as to the amount of money actually subscribed.

5. The Yetter combine has been in control from the first.

After Mr. Young reported to Auditor General Snyder, the latter withheld the regular normal school appropriations. But later this matter was adjusted, and the school received its regular quota, though it remains under the same control.

Date of visit: March 28 and May 4, 1910.

Conclusion.

Such is the story of the management of the so-called state normal schools of Pennsylvania. The picture has not been overdrawn; in fact it does not contain some of the aspects of the real situation.

Fifteen years ago two prominent educators of the State fell into a heated argument as to which one was the author of the Normal School Act of 1857. Very probably to-day neither one would care to be held responsible for the final outcome of this measure. Yet the conditions as they exist to-day could not be found if that act had been legally followed, for, as has been stated elsewhere, this legislative enactment simply laid down a standard of work for a limited number of institutions, which might issue teachers' diplomas and, later, permanent licenses. At that time the state did not give a cent of money or promise to give money to any institution created under this act. Later, certain institutions received aid from the State both before and after meeting the formal requirements. Very soon the State realized it would be necessary to guard the expenditure of the hundreds of thousands of dollars it was annually giving to these

---

[3] The legislature of 1911 has made such expenditures legal.

schools. Then it was discovered that the large stockholders would vigorously oppose every advance the State tried to make to direct how this money should be spent. The best evidence that these private corporations have often fallen into unworthy hands is to be found in this very opposition. If these large share holders were as unselfish and public-spirited as they claim to be, they would be willing and anxious to give these institutions over to the State.

In 1872, the State appointed two trustees; in 1907, the legislature passed an act requiring that nine of the eighteen trustees should be appointed by the state superintendent. Each advance of the state to assume greater control of these institutions has met with much opposition. The protests against the act of 1907 were particularly pronounced in several instances. At the West Chester Normal, the board was reorganized so that the State appointed nine trustees and the stockholders elected nine others. The next year when the litigation arose at West Chester, the defendants and owners of stock contended that the state superintendent did not have the power to appoint nine trustees, and only six were then permitted to serve on the board.

Even if half the trustees are appointed by the state superintendent, the State's interests are scarcely better safe-guarded than they were when but six of the eighteen were appointed. Generally, of course, it is expected that the state superintendent will appoint the state trustees from the list recommended by the stockholders. Seldom does he make appointments on his own initiative; when he does, he must do so " upon the advice and consent of the governor," which is another complication, and of course every complication acts in favor of the small group of stockholders who have been in control.

Occasionally when the state superintendent does make outside appointments, as he did at Mansfield last year (1909) and at Edinboro both this and last year (1910 and 1909), it means friction and loss of friendship for those who were asked to represent the state. Under such conditions a weak man soon succumbs, while a strong man discovers that he has much difficulty in accomplishing anything. Often the weak man is taken over into the fold of the normal school group while the strong man finally becomes disgusted and refuses to serve longer. In the end, whenever one of these contests has developed, two or three men owning a majority of the stock have found themselves without opposition, and the old conditions have continued with but little interruption.

It may be argued that the quarterly reports to the Auditor General's office and the inspection of the books every three or four months by a traveling auditor for the state will be sufficient to prevent irregularities. Anyone who is familiar with the complicated system of bookkeeping in any one of these large school corporations knows that such reports and such examinations are able to interrupt but not to prevent unwise use of funds. Certainly these reports and inspections do not put a stop to clique and bank control, which means that the state's money is frequently wasted and the good the school is able to do is minimized.

Practically all the leading educators of the state, cognizant of the normal school management, are convinced that the present method of control is futile and wrong. Such men as Principals Phillips, Lyte, and Smith, have publicly advocated that the State normal schools should be under the control and direction of a carefully selected professional board, appointed by the governor or the state superintendent. The late Theodore B. Noss, of the California normal, who had enough faith in himself and his profession to spend two years abroad in study, very earnestly advocated this change. Undoubtedly the state will very soon adopt this policy.[4]

One conclusion seems to follow inevitably from this examination of conditions in the Pennsylvania normal schools. Either the system has actually resulted in strife and conflict in the management of the institutions, always to the detriment of their educational work, or a small group, frequently of no more than two or three or a half dozen men, have acquired control. In the latter case private interests have contaminated the service which should be rendered solely in the public interest. In one or two cases selfish private interest has produced open scandal, and in still others openly expressed public suspicion. Such conditions will always make it impossible for any school where they exist to train high-minded and efficient teachers. If the spirit

---

[4] Partial provisions have been made for state ownership in the school laws of 1911.

of a school is morally unsound, those who fall under its influence cannot but be touched, even if unconsciously, by its baneful effects.

Let it not be forgotten also that the very worst condition existing, or that has existed, in any of the schools, is a danger that threatens every school in the state. They are all alike private schools, largely aided by state subvention. To this policy of management may be traced most of the evils to be found in the normal schools of Pennsylvania.

CHAPTER IV

THE ENTRANCE REQUIREMENTS

During the past decade or two, entrance requirements to practically all the professions have been steadily raised. This is especially true of medicine. Only a few years ago, probably not more than fifteen, many of the more prosperous medical schools admitted students from the common schools. At that time the great majority of the schools had a two-year course. Gradually, however, the entrance requirements in many of the better medical institutions were raised and only students that had been graduated from a three-year or four-year high school were admitted, and at the same time the medical course was lengthened to three years. To-day none has less than a four-year course, and many require from one to four years of college work in addition to the four years of high school study. The advance that has been made in medical education has been approached by the best law schools of the country; and to-day many states have high entrance requirements in dentistry, pharmacy, and even veterinary surgery.

In certain states the requirements for entering the teaching profession have in a measure kept pace with those of the other professions, though in a great majority the standards for teaching are lamentably low and unworthy. The states that have done the most to make teaching truly professional are New York, Massachusetts, Indiana, California, and New Jersey. In most of these only graduates of four-year high schools are permitted to become students in the state normals; in fact the requirements are identical with those for entrance to the universities and the colleges of the country. With these higher requirements, which necessarily lead to better preparation on the part of the teachers, the salaries have been increased and the school term lengthened. Indications are that the teaching profession will be placed on a still higher level in the near future. Even in the south, handicapped in its finances and burdened with the other heavy problems, vigorous steps have been taken recently to raise the professional standards for the teachers in both the grades and the high schools.

The condition in Pennsylvania, which is surpassed only by New York in wealth and population, is far from satisfactory. The management of practically all the Pennsylvania state normal schools has kept miserably low standards. Because of the unlimited and indiscriminate " state aid," a premium has been placed upon gross numbers and the standard set in Pennsylvania forty years ago among these state institutions has remained the standard up to the present time. No normal school principal would be continued long in office if he were not able to have a large enrollment in his school. The local boards of trustees know little about the academic and professional work; they do not claim to be educational experts; but they are able to multiply and subtract, and they are instantly opposed to the adoption of any standard that will reduce the numbers and consequently the amount of " state aid." Before the spring of 1910, when the course of study was changed and certain very limited requirements agreed upon at a meeting of the normal school principals, little or no attention was given to the previous preparation of entering students. All were welcome,—the retarded pupil in the grades, the discontented pupil in the first year of high school, and the graduate of a four-year high school course. It is evident that with these indiscriminate qualifications, uniform and satisfactory work was impossible, and as the standard became lower and lower the better qualified pupils were not attracted.

The law of 1866 granted " state aid " to students seventeen years of age and above who studied the science and art of teaching; and at the end of the normal course the state gave an additional reward of $50 to each graduate who promised to teach two years in the public schools. In 1901 the legislature increased the " state aid " to $1.50 a week without laying down a single educational qualification. Many evils have followed in the wake of this age requirement. Since their establishment, practically every normal school has had a preparatory or sub-junior class to which are admitted boys and girls who often are not able to keep pace with their classmates in the common schools or high schools. These individuals are attracted to the normals in order to take the special courses offered or to qualify themselves in the least possible time and with the least possible effort to receive a permanent certificate to teach in the public schools. Regardless of the advancement these pupils make, as soon as they reach the age of seventeen they are enrolled in the " Methods " class so that the school may receive $1.50 a week for their professional preparation. Not all of these individuals keep their promise of teaching. Probably the state loses less if they do not; but whether they do or not, the dullards and the incompetents receive a permanent license and enter into competition with the brightest young men and women in the state.

The incompetents can find no other haven so comfortable and lucrative, and they are able and willing to work for less money than those who see other avenues where competition is more severe and rewards are greater. Eventually, this system discourages and drives out the more capable ones; and the so-called teacher's profession is left largely in the hands of people lacking in scholarship and initiative. The most competent teachers are not sufficiently protected by the minimum salary laws of the state.

It must not be inferred that a majority of the students in the normal schools are not earnest and energetic; such is not the case. A large number of them are studious and capable, though very deficient in academic preparation. Unfortunately, these persons remain in the profession only a short time since they are compelled to stand upon the economic level established by the incompetent class turned out by these institutions.

This indiscriminate giving of state money to privately controlled normal schools offers a temptation for gain, and the principals have been forced into a competition for mere numbers. Under such conditions it is not surprising that these educators have been unable to agree upon any entrance requirements. This has led to an intolerable condition, which can be described in the words of a former principal who said that a Pennsylvania normal school is " an institution for teaching almost any body almost any thing." This statement is quoted from the late Theodore B. Noss, of the California normal school, who was pleading for higher entrance requirements and more co-operation between the normal schools and high schools of Pennsylvania.

Passages will be quoted from both old and new catalogues

of the Pennsylvania normal schools to prove that these institutions have had no entrance requirements worthy of the name. A number of the prominent educators of Pennsylvania will be quoted to show that they realize that the conditions are deplorable and that a radical reform is necessary.

In 1886, the West Chester normal school catalogue contains this statement: " Pupils will be allowed to enter the regular course at any point for which they are actually fitted. They may enter at any time during the session, and will be charged only from date of entrance."

Practically the same statement can be found in the Shippensburg catalogue from 1887 to 1896. Between 1890 and 1897 the Lock Haven catalogues announce that " Students can enter at any time and find profitable work. But it is always better to be present at the opening of the term.

" No examination is required in order to be admitted to the Junior class. Applicants for admission will be assigned to such classes as are suited to their degree of advancement."

The Millersville catalogues from 1890 to 1894 state that " Students will be admitted to the school at any time," with the additional statement that " When students enter school they will be assigned to the class in which their qualifications entitle them to be placed."

The California normal as late as 1896-1897 announced that a student was " prepared to enter here " after having had " the usual course in the common schools at home." It also advises the student to come at once if he desires to save " both time and money." In 1900 the East Stroudsburg catalogue has this rather flexible entrance requirement: " Those who are fairly well advanced in the English branches, by entering the beginning of the Fall term, can complete the work of the Junior year in three terms. . . . On entering, the applicant is placed in such class or classes as his attainment and ability warrant."

Practically every one of the Pennsylvania normal schools admits students to the various classes almost at any time during the year. The Bloomsburg catalogue of 1906-1907 states that " Students in nearly all subjects can be accommodated, even in the middle of the term."

All the announcements for 1908-1909 and 1909-1910 indicate

that the entrance requirements have not been raised. A student might enter any normal school from the grades or the common schools, and be graduated after three years of work. If the standards of New York and Massachusetts were strictly applied to him upon graduation, he would not yet be able to enter a state normal in either of these states until he had studied for a year in a first class high school.

The Lock Haven catalogue for 1908-1909 states that " a good High School course or its equivalent will admit to the Junior class." In January, 1910, two students from the Sophomore class of the Lock Haven High School were admitted upon examination to the Junior year without condition. At the end of two years these individuals (two girls) will receive state diplomas or licenses at the time their former classmates are graduating from the local high school. Pupils from the eighth grade at Lock Haven have been admitted without examination to the sub-junior class. This enables them to become teachers in four years. The situation here is not worse than in many of the other state institutions.

A former principal states that " no examinations worthy of the name have ever been given to students applying for entrance to any normal school of the state. Boys of eleven, and girls even younger are admitted to the various classes to the detriment of the standard of the schools. These individuals are not qualified by mental development or previous preparation to enter the classes with young men and women who are really fitted for professional work." The present director of the model school of one of the normal schools asserts that " Most of these institutions have fallen into the snare of allowing practically anybody to enter the Junior year; and once entered, it is difficult to keep unfit ones from graduating." One of the most competent teachers in another school states that " The preparation of our students upon entering is much varied. A few come well prepared; others are very poorly prepared. It has been customary in the past to accept marks from schools in the districts—High Schools so named—but for several years now we give them an examination, a very easy test, and if they show any signs of knowledge we pass them on.

" Now this matter of credits is a most difficult problem. You know the condition of our high schools. There are six or eight first rate ones in our district. Students from these are fairly well prepared, but the difficulty is to know where to draw the line. The principals of the smaller schools, which are not high schools in any real sense, say, ' If you do not accept our marks, we will send our graduates to schools that do,' and they keep their word. The marks we get are no index at all of the pupils' ability. The grades presented to us range from 90 per cent to 100 per cent. I have just examined a dozen students in General History. The lowest grade presented to me was 90 per cent, the highest 99 per cent. These students had this work in class last year. Here are the questions I gave them for the entrance examination:

    1. Tell what you can about the Peloponnesian war.

    2. Point out differences in character between the Athenians and the Spartans.

    3. What were the causes and results of the War of the Roses?

    4. What were the following:

        (a)   The Renaissance.

        (b)   The German Reformation.

        (c)   The Hundred Years' War.

        (d)   The Peace of Westphalia.

" If I had graded the papers of these students according to the standards I used to follow in high school, their marks would have ranged between 30 per cent and 70 per cent. As it was I passed them all. You notice that the character of the questions is quite different from that of the questions I would give in a regular examination; these are general and strike only the mountain peaks.

" The preparation of our students in the common school branches is deplorable. These individuals come largely from country schools, but even those from the graded schools are wretchedly prepared. They have no accurate knowledge, and their examinations show a miserable hodge-podge. After they come to us, our patchy course of study—24 weeks for General History—makes the situation still more miserable. We have been told that this century is a time of rapid transit, but our course of study can hardly be excelled in speed except by the new course which in many respects is still worse."

The above quotations indicate something of the standards that have been employed by all the normal schools. With the adoption of this new course of study in the spring of 1910, the principals laid down the first uniform entrance requirements that the Pennsylvania normal schools have ever agreed upon in the fifty years of their existence. The standard states that " Students admitted to the First Year shall have a fair knowledge of Arithmetic, Reading, Orthography, Penmanship, United States History, Geography, Grammar, Physiology, Civics, and the Elements of Algebra to Quadratics. Test by Faculty." The fact that this requirement has been heralded as an improvement, over the old order where each institution set its own standards seems to justify the severe criticisms that have been made by educators in and out of the state.

The entrance requirements now agreed upon for the Pennsylvania normal schools are no higher than those for admittance to a good New York high school. All the work upon which the entering students will be examined, with the exception of Elementary Algebra, is distinctly of common school grade and no statement is made to the effect that the pupils must be graduated from the common schools. It is not possible to say that the standard has been raised; the matter still rests largely in the hands of each principal. The Preparatory or Sub-Junior class will still be a ready receptacle for all the educational misfits that may apply for admittance from the sixth or seventh grade, and the same laxity in entrance requirements will probably continue in the future. Practically no student, regardless of his age or his preparation, has ever been refused admittance to any normal school in the state. There are few, very few, exceptions to this sweeping statement.

In fact, even if this entrance requirement agreed upon in 1910 is enforced, the standard is low and reward in time saved is offered to those coming directly from the country or graded schools. The pupils may be conditioned in Algebra and one of the elementary branches, but they still have considerably the advantage of pupils from high schools. A reward of two years is given to those who do not spend a single day in the local high school but enter at once one of the state normals. Here are the rules laid down by the principals for admitting pupils from the secondary schools of the state:

"Resolved that properly certified graduates of approved Pennsylvania High Schools of the first grade and city High Schools [four years in length] as listed by the Department of Public Instruction, be recommended to the State Board of Examiners for entrance to the third year of the Four Years' Course of the State Normal Schools without examination by the Faculty, and be conditioned in the branches that have not been satisfactorily completed by such students.

"Resolved that properly certified graduates of approved Pennsylvania High Schools of the second grade [three years in length] be recommended to the State Board of Examiners for entrance to the second year of the Four Years' Course of the State Normal Schools without examination by the faculty, and be conditioned in the branches that have not been satisfactorily completed by such students.

"Resolved that properly certified graduates of approved Pennsylvania High Schools of the third grade [two years in length] be admitted to the first year of the Four Years' Course of the State Normal Schools without examination, and be conditioned in the branches that have not been satisfactorily completed by such students."

The following table will show that the entrance requirements are distinctly in favor of the pupil from the common schools:

TABLE 1

Years in the Common School	Years in High School	Years in Normal School	Total Preparation for permanent certificate
8 years	0	4	12 years
8 years	2	4	14 years
8 years	3	3	14 years
8 years	4	2	14 years

In other words the new course of study is setting a premium upon inefficient and poor preparation and is permitting and even encouraging the state normals to continue their competition against the public high schools. The wording of the above resolutions indicates that the four-year high school graduate will be conditioned in both School Management and School Law and General Methods, so that besides losing two years of time, he is compelled to do additional work during the third and fourth years of the normal course.

Because of the adoption of the four-year curriculum, which requires only a common school preparation, these low standards will be retained. Frequently, the normal school principals are not to blame for this condition of affairs. Back of them stand the local boards of trustees who would instantly resent any action that would tend to reduce the attendance. The succeeding chapter will show how seriously the low entrance requirements affect the curriculum of the normal schools, and how they force these institutions to attempt impossible tasks.

CHAPTER V

THE CURRICULUM

The law of 1857, dividing the state of Pennsylvania into twelve normal school districts (later thirteen), provided that the course of study for the state normal schools should be agreed upon by a majority of the normal school principals and approved by the state superintendent. Almost without exception the normal schools had developed from private academies. The principals of these schools agreed upon three regular courses, two of which were wholly academic, and the other, known as the " Elementary Course," and designed for those who expected to teach in the common schools, gave but little attention to professional instruction. This was quite natural, but none the less unfortunate, since it resulted in an inauguration of the work of the normal schools along cultural, rather than professional lines.

The ultimate result has been that professional studies have been forced to gain admission, whenever admission could be gained at all, by crowding into an already full course. From the standpoint of educational efficiency, the greatest defect of the Pennsylvania normal schools is their overcrowded curriculum. Their work is a jumble of attempts to do what belongs to the sixth, seventh, and eighth grades of the common schools, to the high schools, to the colleges, and to schools for the professional training of teachers. Even at the present day music is a special study in every one of the thirteen schools, and most of them have a formidable array of extras besides, none of which have any bearing upon professional training of teachers, though they are sometimes combined with a nominal attendance upon " methods " lectures, thus making those who are enrolled in them eligible for state aid.

As the original " Elementary Course " at Millersville is the one from which the later normal courses have been evolved, it

46

is best to give it in detail. This course extended only two years above the work of the common schools. Part of the academic subjects were continuations of the common school branches, such as arithmetic (mental and written), penmanship, reading, grammar, and history of the United States. The majority were distinctly high school in character, such as Natural Philosophy, Botany, Rhetoric, Geometry and Plane Trigonometry. One hour a day for a year was devoted to the Theory of Teaching and an hour a day for a half year to Practice Teaching in the Model School.

This Elementary Course is here given:

First Term
Orthography and Etymology
Reading and Elocution
Writing and Drawing
Geography
Mental Arithmetic
Written Arithmetic
Grammar
Vocal Music

Second Term
Reading and Elocution
Writing and Drawing
Physical Geography
Higher Grammar
Elements of Algebra
Physiology
Theory of Teaching
Vocal Music

Third Term
History of the United States
Algebra
Elements of Natural Philosophy
Rhetoric
Geometry (five books)
Theory of Teaching
Bookkeeping

Fourth Term
Geometry Completed and Plane Trigonometry
Elements of Chemistry
Botany or Zoölogy
Practice Teaching

This course was also adopted at Edinboro in 1861 when that institution was officially recognized. Probably no change was made in it until 1866 when the state legislature passed an act,

giving aid to all students over seventeen years of age who signi-
fied their intention of teaching in the common schools of the
state and who " receive regular instruction in the science and
art of teaching in a special class devoted to that object for the
whole time such an allowance is drawn."

In 1870, a few changes were made in the curriculum of the
five state normal schools then in existence. The theory of
teaching was given an hour a day for a year and a half, and
this was followed by an hour a day for a half year of practice
teaching. The only other important change in the curriculum
was made by reducing the time devoted to mathematics: only
part of the work of solid geometry was presented and plane
trigonometry was entirely omitted. This course of study remained in operation until 1880.

In this year, several important changes were made. Less time,
it would seem, was devoted to the common school branches, for
both Grammar and Etymology were dropped out, and Mental
and Written Arithmetic were also omitted. At this meeting the
principals again reduced the time given to higher mathematics,
and the work in solid geometry was dropped. In place of these
subjects, Latin was introduced for the first time, though for but
one year, the work being confined to the study of grammar and
the completion of the first book of Caesar. Some attention was
also given to the English classics, but the main reason for chang-
ing the program at this time was to make room for two professional subjects—School Economy and Mental Philosophy.

Seven years later, in 1887, at another meeting of the normal
school principals and the state superintendent, more Latin was
required though the work was still confined to grammar and
Caesar. The most important change made at this time was in
the additional emphasis that was given to the theory of teaching. Though the course had not yet been extended to three
years, the work in the theory of teaching had been subdivided
so that attention was given to school management, methods, and
psychology; and in addition to these, a short course in the history of education was required.

In 1894, at the end of another seven-year period, two meetings of the normal school principals were called to revise the course of study. At the first meeting several additions were made. Arithmetic and English Grammar, which were in the course of study in 1859, were reintroduced; additional work was prescribed in Caesar; and the new subjects, Manual Training and General History, were added. During this same year, but at a later meeting, the curriculum was radically changed by offering a third year which all students were recommended to take, though not compelled to do so.

The work of the optional year was divided between high school and professional subjects. Solid geometry, plane and analytical trigonometry and surveying were prescribed, and short courses were given in chemistry, zoölogy, and geology. Special work was also offered in English and American literature. Three books of both Caesar and Virgil, and three orations of Cicero were added to the work in Latin prescribed for the elementary course. The pedagogical instruction included psychology, moral science, school supervision, philosophy of education, and methods of teaching.

The addition of this optional year in 1894 for regular normal school students indicates that the normal school principals were not satisfied with the preparation they had been giving their students; and finally, in 1900, they agreed upon a compulsory three-year course for graduation, which consisted of the regular elementary course of two years with the addition of the former optional year. At the same time work in Greek, German, and French, was introduced, and students were permitted to substitute language work for certain courses in science or mathematics; but in most of the normal schools few elected French or Greek and the language work was therefore largely confined to German and Latin. This course of study, adopted in 1900, was divided into the three years, called Junior, Middle, and Senior, and was continued for ten years by the thirteen normal schools. The following division by years and subjects is taken from the catalogue of the Indiana, Pennsylvania, Normal School:

OLD COURSE

FIRST YEAR

Mathematics (Algebra, Arithmetic)...............	260	45 minute periods
Latin......................................	200	" "
Pedagogics (School management)................	137½	" "
Music......................................	48	" "
Drawing....................................	112	" "
United States History and Civics..............	140	" "
Physiology.................................	60	" "
Bookkeeping................................	75	" "
Geography..................................	65	" "
Physical Culture............................	80	" "

1177½

SECOND YEAR

Mathematics (Plane Geometry)..................	140	" "
English (Rhetoric, Composition, Elocution)........	130	" "
Botany.....................................	60	" "
Zoölogy....................................	60	" "
History (General)............................	125	" "
Latin (Caesar)..............................	200	" "
Pedagogics (Psychology, Methods)...............	200	" "
Manual Training.............................	75	" "
Chemistry..................................	140	" "
Physical Culture............................	80	" "

1210

THIRD YEAR

Pedagogics (Methods, Hist. of Ed., Teaching)......	270	" "
Latin (Cicero, Virgil).........................	200	" "
English (Lit. and Classics, review of grammar).....	200	" "
Mathematics (So. Geom., Trig., Surv., review arith.)	260	" "
Physics....................................	140	" "
Geology....................................	60	" "
Physical Culture............................	80	" "

1210

Very shortly after the adoption of the three-year course of study in 1900, several of the normal school principals advocated radical changes. The objections by these educators were numerous enough, but somewhat conflicting: some insisted that the course of study should be reduced to two years in length, and be confined entirely to professional and semi-professional studies; others contended that the course should be lengthened in order to give opportunity for more thorough work. Of the remaining principals two or three were indifferent, while one or two were defenders of the course as it stood.

In writing to the State Superintendent in 1907, one normal school principal stated "that the course of study is too extensive to make possible the thorough drill in the fundamental studies that is so necessary to the success as a teacher of the common schools." This indicates that at least one principal favored a smaller number of academic studies and more attention to review and drill work in the common school subjects. At the same time Principal Lyte of Millersville made the assertion that " some Normal Schools are obstacles in the way of establishing high schools, because they themselves attempt to do work of second or third grade high schools and thus prevent the establishment of high schools." Principal Kemp of the East Stroudsburg normal school, in his report to the state superintendent in 1909, stated that "the academic work in the last two years is entirely too heavy, and crowds out much needed professional work. A number of the studies in the middle and senior years are nothing more than high school studies that should be well taken care of before the middle year is reached. . . . The junior year is no better than the last year in a good grammar school and it should really be at least equal to the third year in a good high school." Doctor Theodore B. Noss, the late principal of the California normal school, also contended that the course of study should be modified, giving less attention to high school subjects and much more attention to the professional preparation of teachers. Finally in the spring of 1910, after two or three protracted and rather heated conferences, a four-year course was agreed upon. It is given here with prefatory explanations as made out by the principals at their final conference:

" This course is based on the ' unit ' plan as proposed by the Carnegie Foundation.

"A unit represents a year's study in any subject in a secondary school constituting approximately a quarter of a full year's work.

" This statement is designed to afford a standard of measurement for the work done in secondary schools. It takes the four-year High School Course as a basis and assumes that the length of the school year is from thirty-six to forty weeks, that a period is from forty to sixty minutes in length and that the study is pursued for four or five periods a week; but, under ordinary circumstances, a satisfactory year's work in any subject cannot be accomplished in less than one hundred and twenty sixty-minute hours or their equivalent. Schools organized on a different basis can nevertheless estimate their work in terms of this unit.

" Students admitted to the First Year shall have a fair knowledge of Arithmetic, Reading, Orthography, Penmanship, United States History, Geography, Grammar, Physiology, Civics, and the Elements of Algebra to Quadratics.   Test by Faculty."

FIRST YEAR

Algebra	160	45 minute periods
Latin	160	" "
School Management and School Law	160	" "
Orthography	40	" "
Reading and Public Speaking	50	" "
Ancient and Mediaeval History	100	" "
Physical Geography	50	" "
Arithmetic	100	" "
Grammar	160	" "
Vocal Music	50	" "
Physical Training	80	" "
Manual Training or Domestic Science	50	" "
	1160	

SECOND YEAR

Plane Geometry	160	" "
Rhetoric, Composition and Classics	160	" "
Botany	100	" "
Zoölogy	50	" "
Bookkeeping	50	" "
Modern History and English History	100	" "
Caesar (Four Books)	160	" "
General Methods	160	" "
Drawing	100	" "
Physical Training	80	" "
Manual Training or Domestic Science	50	" "
	1170	

THIRD YEAR

Psychology and Observation	160	" "
Cicero or German or French	160	" "
Literature, English and American	100	" "
History, U. S. and Civics	80	" "
Geography	80	" "
Physiology and School Sanitation	80	" "
Solid Geometry and Trigonometry	160	" "
Methods in History and Geography	100	" "
Physics	160	" "
Physical Training	80	" "
	1160	

Substitutions Offered: History of Arts and Sciences, French or German for Cicero.   French, German, or Geology and Astronomy for Solid Geometry and Trigonometry.

FOURTH YEAR

		45 minute periods
Practice Teaching	160	
Observation or Plan Work, Practice must be at least	100	20 " "
History of Education	100	45 " "
Agriculture and Nature Study	160	" "
Arithmetic	50	" "
Grammar	50	" "
Methods in Arithmetic and Grammar	100	" "
Virgil (Six Books), German or French	160	" "
Public Speaking	50	" "
Chemistry	160	" "
Drawing	50	" "
Manual Training or Domestic Science	50	" "
Physical Training	80	" "
	1110	

Substitutions Offered: French, German, (Ethics, Logic and Sociology), or, (Philosophy of Education and Surveying) for Virgil. Note—Surveying may take the place of either Ethics, Logic or Sociology.

Of the 3597 hours given under the three-year course, 2397 were devoted to what can rightly be called high school subjects, and 353 to common school branches. Exclusive of physical training, this leaves 607½ hours for professional studies, or 18½ per cent of the entire time. The revised course has 2750 hours for high school subjects and 540 for common school branches, with 990 left for professional study, or 23 per cent of the entire time.

These figures lead to the conclusion that the new course of study is not an improvement over the old one. In fact, no radical change has been made; the additional year has simply proportionately increased the time devoted to each phase of the work: 382½ hours to the professional side; 353 to high school subjects, and 187 to the common school branches. In the old curriculum the work, exclusive of the time for physical training, required 27.97 recitations per week or 5½ per day. Little improvement has been made in the new four-year course since it requires 26.75 recitations per week or 5⅓ per day.

One of the weaknesses of the curriculum is a result of the limited time and emphasis given to the subject of English composition and literature. Practically one-third of this entire time is devoted to grammar and 40 periods are assigned to spelling. This leaves not more than 360 periods to the English work as it is given in a modern high school. Most of these precious 360 recitations are given to the discussion of two or three classics and to the lives of noted authors. Oral and written composition receive very little attention.

The English teacher has all he can do to prepare for six or seven recitation periods a day; he has left neither energy nor time to correct essays, and the students are too busy going from one class to another to devote much time to any one study.

During any year of a first-class high school the pupils write more essays than do the normal students in three or four years. The oral composition work is generally left in the hands of the Elocution teacher, who is busy with a small group, rehearsing for a play or other public performance. As a consequence, the students often show skill in analysing sentences, although they are not able to write or speak their native language with correctness and ease. They hear much about the "theme" of a selection, but at the end of the normal course they have little or no appreciation of the best literature. When the normal school students go out to teach in the grammar grades and the smaller high schools of the state, it is very evident that the English work, the core of the curriculum, cannot be well taught. As a consequence, each succeeding school generation shows to what an alarming extent a crowded normal school curriculum can directly injure the common schools of the state.

The number of hours devoted to academic work in the Pennsylvania normal schools and in the first class high schools is practically the same. In the former case the total number of hours given to academic study (high school and common school) is 3290, while in the latter all of the 3458 hours are given to the high school studies. The difference of 168 hours is insignificant. This similarity is made still more evident by comparing the number of recitations per week or day required in each instance. The high school course requires less than 23 per week or 4.55 per day, while the academic side of the normal school curriculum requires 20.5 hours per week or 4.1 per day. If the academic work of the Pennsylvania normal schools is well done, is there any room for the 990 additional hours required for professional study?

CHAPTER VI

ADVERTISING METHODS AND SPECIAL COURSES

An investigation of the advertising methods employed by practically all the Pennsylvania normal schools shows at once the principal reason why the entrance requirements are very low and why the curriculum is crowded and unsatisfactory. The creation of the many special courses of study indicates to what extent the demand for gross numbers has distorted the aim of these professional schools. The effect of this desire for students has been far-reaching and it will not cease until the state takes the control of its normal schools out of the hands of private corporations and of men who are indifferent to the purpose for which these institutions were established.

Mention has already been made of the prevalence of wholly unprofessional " special studies," and of the indefensible custom of combining such studies with " methods " classes in order to make students of music, or bookkeeping, or photography eligible for state aid.

Many students enrolled in these special courses do not expect to teach. A few, refusing to accept " state aid " under false pretenses, pay their own tuition, including additional fees. However, many others do not hesitate to let the state pay sixty dollars a year for their education in stenography, bookkeeping, music, art and oratory. The " state aid " is frequently more than enough to pay the tuition for many of these special courses. If it is not, the school makes a deduction to those pupils who take " Methods " and ask for " State aid "; in such an event, the student pays less than he would otherwise and the school receives considerably more.

Because of the profit derived from these special courses, it is easily understood why a majority of the Pennsylvania state normal schools have become institutions " for teaching almost anybody almost anything."

Certain of these institutions employ as teachers men who are in demand in the county institutes of the state, and who have consequently great influence in attracting young men and women to their schools. Such lecturers are permitted to leave the normals for an afternoon or evening address two or three times a week, and even to spend as much as ten or twelve weeks in county institutes, though these are held during the school term. The class work of these men, which is of much greater importance, necessarily suffers, but the attendance in the normal schools is increased by this plan of advertising.

A great deal of attention is given to athletics, since these schools have discovered, as did the colleges twenty years ago, that it increases the attendance to have a winning foot-ball or base-ball team. Several of the state normals have splendid gymnasiums while their libraries are small and thoroughly inadequate and their model schools are poorly furnished and unsatisfactory. Shippensburg, for instance, has both a new gymnasium and athletic field with a grand-stand, while its training school is in cramped and unsatisfactory quarters, and its library is very small. At Edinboro, the science building is wholly inadequate, with miserable equipment, but the school has both an athletic field and an attractive gymnasium. The library at Lock Haven, although it has been improved and enlarged in the past two years, is still lacking in space and volumes. The gymnasium, however, is one of the features of the school. Kutztown has one of the finest gymnasiums in the State, but its library room, which contains few modern books, is very small and it has no experienced librarian to direct the students in their readings.

In the central and western parts of the State, the normal schools send out " educational runners " to increase the enrollment. These agents go from town to town and village to village, calling upon the older pupils in the country schools and the boys and girls in the eighth grade and in the first year of high school. Often the competition becomes so heated that charges for board and room are reduced. The agent, however, has generally discovered that his strongest appeal to the parents is to show them that their son or daughter can save a year's time in obtaining a permanent teacher's certificate by attending the school he is advertising; while his strongest appeal to the prospective pupils is to emphasize the attractions of the student life,—the athletic events, the social affairs, the freedom granted to all, and a minimum of distasteful and difficult work.

The condition in the eastern part of the State is similar though the advertising methods are somewhat different. In some respects, the contest is fiercer since the schools in the east are more closely located. The alumni of each normal are called upon to send students to the school, and occasionally the campaigning methods require the head of the normal school to give his personal attention to prospective students.

CHAPTER VII

THE STATE BOARD EXAMINATIONS

For many years the State Board Examinations held at the Pennsylvania normal schools at the end of each academic year have failed in their purpose. Few educators in the state will defend them, and many school men do not hesitate to say that they are not only useless, but also dangerous, since they encourage poor work and permit an evasion of the spirit of the law relating to the certification of teachers.

As early as 1859 the law provided for the examination of those students who were recommended for graduation by " the whole faculty ", it required that this examination be conducted by not less than three principals ("of whom the principal of the school whose students are to be examined shall be one ") and stipulated that the Superintendent of Common Schools be present in person. Later these requirements were changed to a certain extent; the number of principals on the board was reduced to two, and the Superintendent was permitted to send a deputy, and to enlarge the board by the appointment of from two to six city, county, borough or township superintendents. Up to 1901, these examinations were given only to the graduating classes, but at that time the principals, with the consent of the State Superintendent, agreed that all the students in the regular classes should come under this jurisdiction and be examined by the boards not only for graduation but also for promotion to a higher class. As a consequence, these state board examinations affect most of the students in the regular classes, and much of the burden of maintaining standards of scholarship is shifted upon these few men who come to the institutions at the end of the academic year to remain but two or three days. In the past as few as four or five men have been in charge of an examination, and in two or three days these men were supposed to grade four or five thousand papers, and examine hundreds of notebooks,—a physical impossibility. The number of examiners has recently been increased and the time somewhat extended, but the situation is still far from satisfactory.

Much might be said concerning the educational qualifications and the experience of some of the men that are chosen for this important duty, but that is unnecessary since the limited time and the enormous task make it impossible for the most competent and conscientious to do their work well. In fact, these examinations enable an ambitious school principal to coerce his faculty into approving many students that should not be passed under any circumstances. As a result, these persons often slip through because of the overwork or carelessness of an examiner, and thereby the educational standard of the state is seriously affected.

To show just how much of a farce these examinations are it is sufficient to know that one normal school principal claims that no student in his school has failed in a state board examination in twenty-three years. Another principal has a clear record for twenty years. Such information is given a prominent place in the chapel talks, in the official letters written to prospective students, and in the various publications sent out to advertise the institution. Since the principal whose students are being examined is an official member of the board, it is very easy for him to save many who otherwise would be failed, and occasionally he does not hesitate to protest most vigorously against conditioning or failing a single one of his students. In all fairness, however, it should be stated that two or three of the Pennsylvania normal school principals do not ask their faculties to endorse doubtful students; neither do they try to save the record of the school by begging an examiner to withdraw his objections to one of their students, who has done poorly in the final test. Principal Rothermel, of the Kutztown normal school, is one of the men who assume this attitude. But even then this system is undesirable since it tends to lessen and divide responsibility rather than increase and concentrate it; and seldom or never does it really assist a school to maintain a reasonably high standard of scholarship.

The following description by a prominent educator of the state, who is at present a normal school teacher, will indicate the attitude and opinion of the majority of Pennsylvania educators toward these examinations:

" The state board examinations are a farce to some extent. Too much credit is given to the school record of applicants for state diplomas. Because these examinations are superficial in so many cases, the principal coerces his faculty to pass students who are not quite prepared. He believes the student will get the benefit of the doubt and such is the case. As a consequence there is no check by either the faculty or the examining board. The attitude of this principal is not different from that of a majority of the heads of the normal schools of the state. The moral effect upon the students and their work is very bad since they know the principal will step in at the end and induce his faculty to recommend many individuals who do not deserve the state diploma."

Another account written by an efficient educator it is impossible to give in full. It is a complete description of what occurred during the three days a board was in session at one of the normal schools. However, the following extracts can be given without revealing his identity:

" We arrived at . . . . late Monday evening, and Tuesday afternoon went out to the normal school and held a few examinations. That night two of us sat up together until three o'clock correcting papers. Wednesday we examined all day and Wednesday night we sat up until five o'clock correcting papers. Thursday morning I held my last examination which was in . . . ., getting through a little before twelve o'clock. At twelve the examiners met, and I did not have time to look over more than six or eight of the sixty papers written that morning.

" The other examiner, who had spent as much time as I had in trying to go over carefully the papers of the students, found as many as fifty papers that showed a miserable lack of scholarship. In my examination of the papers, I found practically the same persons to have failed. Twenty of these were seniors who expected to receive in a few days a diploma which would be changed in two years to a life certificate. Because of the poor spelling, the miserable English, and the mis-statement of facts not a single one of these twenty should have been passed. This other examiner, who had conscientiously read the papers, agreed with me that these persons should not be granted diplomas under any circumstances. We asked for the class records of these students; they were produced, showing that the students had in the main done poor work in school. But after some wrangling among the members of the board which ended finally with a fervent appeal by the principal who explained that he had never in his life protested against the passing of students in other normal schools where he had been on the examining board, we were practically forced to give up, and this we did as gracefully as we could. As a consequence, no other examiner protested against promoting or graduating a single student in that school. Yet I am sure that all the examiners believed that no injustice would have been done if 25% of the students recommended by the faculty of that school had been failed.

" This is not an exceptional case. I have been a member of other boards, and what occurred in this school has seemingly occurred all too frequently in every other Pennsylvania normal school.

" Sometimes the examiners do not perform their duties at all. I have known one to play tennis during the examination days all the while; and I have heard of others that gave themselves up to the social group they met at the hotel or in a lodge.

" Frequently the questions are highly impractical. In a Latin examination, I have known the longest and most intricate indirect discourse to be offered first-year students out of its context; or vocabularies to be offered from texts which the students never saw. Even then the students were passed; the examiner probably did not know that the questions he put showed clearly to all school men that he was incompetent to grade Latin papers. Is it any wonder that the state board examinations have been considered a mere form? "

From the foregoing it is very clear that the influence of the lay boards of control is as unfortunate in the state examinations as in other departments of normal school activities. If a principal attempted to raise his standard of scholarship for promotion and graduation, he would find that many of his weaker students would leave and go to another institution where the former low standard is maintained; and of course as a result, the principal would have to report to his board that the attendance had fallen off. If he were perfectly frank with his trustees and explained the reason for this, he would soon discover that his official life was in jeopardy, his salary cut, and his faculty reduced. The lay board knows little about educational standards, but it knows a good deal about the difficulty of maintaining an unprofitable plant.

CHAPTER VIII
THE STUDENT BODY

The future of the public schools of Pennsylvania has depended and will continue to depend to a large extent upon the product of the state normal schools. Most educational reforms come from above: the college stimulates the work of the high school, and the high school, generally speaking, evaluates and strengthens the work of the common schools. The Pennsylvania state normal schools are more numerous than those of any other state; they have, therefore, occupied in a small measure the place of a state university in directing and modifying the entire system of schools, both secondary and elementary. In fact they have been looked upon as the standardizing force in the educational field.

The teaching profession must require thorough preparation of its members if it is to rank with medicine, engineering, dentistry and the other professions which demand for entrance many years of academic and professional study.

A careful examination has been made of the eighty-five hundred students enrolled during the year 1909-1910 in the thirteen Pennsylvania state normal schools. Of these, 3950 were questioned directly in their classrooms, and the facts thus obtained have been supplemented and verified by office records when such records were kept. The information received indicates whether the preparatory work of the students was obtained in country or town schools; it also gives the sex, age, and teaching experience of the students, in addition to the amount of their previous academic work and the number of daily recitations they must take to complete the course in the stipulated time.

This examination has shown that most of the normal students are products of the country and village schools; probably less than thirty per cent are from even the smaller cities of the state. Of the four thousand students personally questioned, forty-nine per cent were reared in the country and attended the country schools.

The chapter on the entrance requirements for these normal schools shows that a considerable reward in time is offered to students with no high school preparation. As a consequence,

62

but 11.9 per cent of the 3572 students in the three regular classes in the year 1909-1910 had a full four-year high school course; 17.6 per cent had only three years in secondary schools, and 44 per cent had no work whatever above the common schools before entering the normal schools.

The information gathered as to the number of daily recitations bears out the statement made in the chapter on the curriculum to the effect that such a course of study could be completed in the stipulated time only if the students were required to take an impossible number of recitations. Of the 3572 students questioned, 37.8 per cent had six, and 36.4 per cent had from seven to nine daily recitations requiring definite preparation. In addition, the students were compelled to take courses in music, drawing and physical training. One of the experienced and well-educated Pennsylvania normal school teachers has this to say about the number of daily recitations:

" The course provides that students shall take about six studies per day, a fact that makes anything beyond the most superficial work impossible. But the evil does not stop here. Scores of students are permitted to take seven, eight, or even nine, lessons per day. This condition is worse in the case of the students who try to do the work of both the Junior and Middle-year classes in one year. During the past school session over fifty such students have had nine lessons per day. Such a practice is absolutely indefensible and should be condemned in the strongest terms."

The condition this teacher describes is to be found in nearly every normal school. For instance, 79 students at West Chester, over 80 at Indiana and over 250 at Millersville completed both the Junior and Middle years during the school year of 1909-1910 and were candidates for graduation in June, 1911. At East Stroudsburg, 25 students were given diplomas after one year's residence. Many of these persons have taught on provisional certificates and some have had two, three, or four years' work in some of the Pennsylvania high schools; but it is impossible to believe that they have done thorough work. If the regular students are compelled to carry an abnormal number of subjects, it is evident that those attempting to do two years in one cannot do the work satisfactorily. The fact that the Pennsylvania normal schools will annually permit several hundred of their students to do two years in one is incontestable proof that these institutions have low standards of scholarship and that they send out few students that have acquired true habits of study or understand the difference between thorough and slip-shod work. Is it possible for these students as teachers to require thorough work from their pupils in the public schools?

The following table,—Table 2,—gives the data of the Juniors as to previous academic preparation:

TABLE 2.—Giving facts concerning the Juniors in ten Pennsylvania normal schools for 1909–1910 as to the amount of previous high school work.

Name of School	Total number reporting	Percentage having had 1 year of high school work	Percentage having had 2 years of high school work	Percentage having had 3 years of high school work	Percentage having had 4 years of high school work	Percentage from private schools	Percentage having had from 1 to 4 years of high school work	Percentage having had no high school work
California.......	177	25.4	5.6	3.4	0	5.6	40.0	60.0
Clarion.........	97	17.5	13.4	3.1	1.0	2.1	37.1	62.9
Edinboro........	50	24.0	12.0	2.0	0	0	38.0	62.0
Indiana.........	48	18.75	18.75	18.75	10.42	0	66.66	33.33
Kutztown.......	184	10.3	12.0	8.2	1.6	0.5	32.6	67.4
Lock Haven.....	119	1.7	6.7	10.1	15.1	3.4	37.0	63.0
Millersville......	126	5.6	27.0	24.6	10.3	0.8	68.3	31.7
Shippensburg....	86	9.3	13.9	12.8	0	3.5	39.5	60.5
Slippery Rock...	146	12.3	8.9	8.2	2.1	0	31.5	68.5
West Chester....	132	12.9	15.2	18.9	4.5	*	51.5	48.5

* Number from private schools at West Chester are included with those having had high school work.

The above table shows that few of the Juniors in the Pennsylvania normal schools for 1909-1910 have attended a secondary school for a considerable length of time. With the exception of Indiana, Millersville, and West Chester, more than 60 per cent of the Juniors have had no high school work, and in nearly every instance the majority of those students from high schools have had but one or two years. As has been explained elsewhere, the word high school means little in the smaller communities of Pennsylvania, for in many places a ninth grade of the common schools has been known as a high school.

If these junior students had been enrolled in a good secondary school, they would have had to carry four or five daily studies requiring definite preparation. In the normal schools, practically none of the students had as few as four daily recitations; in fact, in only three of the above ten schools do even one-third carry as few as five studies, while most of them have seven or eight daily recitations. The exceptions to this statement are few, for only at Clarion, California, Indiana and West Chester do less than twenty-five per cent have seven or eight. In all the other six schools, from 52 to 88.1 per cent of the Juniors carry from seven to nine daily recitations requiring definite preparation. These students are asked to do twice as much as they would be permitted to do in a good high school.

The following table, Table 3, gives facts for the normal school students in the second or middle year with respect to previous academic preparation:

TABLE 3.—Giving facts concerning the middle-year class in ten Pennsylvania state normal schools for 1909–1910 as to the amount of previous high school work.

Name of School	Total number reporting	Percentage having had 1 year of high school work	Percentage having had 2 years of high school work	Percentage having had 3 years of high school work	Percentage having had 4 years of high school work	Percentage from private schools	Percentage having had from 1 to 4 years of high school work	Percentage having had no high school work
California.......	154	18.2	17.5	14.9	3.9	6.5	61.0	39.0
Clarion..........	85	5.9	24.7	16.5	16.5	1.1	64.7	35.3
Edinboro........	82	9.7	35.4	14.6	4.9	0	64.6	35.4
Indiana.........	90	4.4	20.0	21.1	23.3	2.2	71.0	29.0
Kutztown.......	174	5.7	18.4	20.1	13.2	0.6	58.0	42.0
Lock Haven.....	97	0	10.3	13.4	16.5	7.2	47.4	52.6
Millersville......	102	9.8	11.8	11.8	26.4	1.0	60.8	39.2
Shippensburg....	52	15.4	7.7	13.4	2.0	2.0	40.5	59.5
Slippery Rock...	102	7.8	21.6	22.5	4.0	0	55.9	44.1
West Chester....	266	6.7	19.2	28.6	23.3	*	77.8	22.2

* Number from private schools at West Chester are included with those having had high school work.

A comparison of this and Table No. 2 shows that a larger percentage of these students have had four years in a secondary school, and a considerably larger proportion have completed a three-year course. Many of these students were given advanced standing.

These students also had an abnormal number of studies though less Middlers than Juniors had from seven to nine recitations. The percentage who carried this large number of recitations varies considerably since but 10.7 per cent at Clarion had so many, while at Kutztown 60.7, and at Shippensburg 65.4 per cent had from seven to nine recitations. If all those students who took in one year the work of the Junior and Middle years had been included, this table would show a great increase in the abnormal number of recitations, since, for instance, of the 246 Junior-Middlers at Millersville over 77 per cent had from seven to nine daily recitations, and practically all the seventy-nine Junior-Middlers at West Chester had nine recitations.

The following table, Table 4, gives the facts for the Seniors in eleven of these normal schools as to previous academic preparation:

TABLE 4.—Giving facts concerning the Seniors in eleven of the Pennsylvania state normal schools for 1909–1910 as to the amount of previous high school work.

Name of School	Total number reporting	Percentage having had 1 year of high school work	Percentage having had 2 years of high school work	Percentage having had 3 years of high school work	Percentage having had 4 years of high school work	Percentage from private schools	Percentage having had from 1 to 4 years of high school work	Percentage having had no high school work
Bloomsburg (over ½ Senior class) .	91	5.5	12.0	18.6	20.9	4.6	61.6	38.4
California.......	146	8.9	15.0	12.3	10.3	5.5	52.0	48.0
Clarion.........	75	5.0	23.0	7.0	12.0	1.0	48.0	52.0
Edinboro........	117	1.5	25.0	13.0	11.0	0	64.0	36.0
Indiana.........	81	2.5	13.6	14.8	25.9	3.7	60.5	39.5
Kutztown.......	141	4.0	12.0	30.0	7.0	1.0	54.0	46.0
Lock Haven.....	70	8.6	11.4	30.0	14.3	8.6	72.9	27.1
Millersville......	113	4.4	11.5	38.0	23.9	1.8	79.6	20.4
Shippensburg....	67	1.5	10.5	16.4	14.9	1.5	44.8	55.2
Slippery Rock...	91	6.6	11.0	13.2	20.9	1.1	42.8	47.2
West Chester....	211	4.7	14.2	35.5	20.9	*	75.3	24.7

* Number from private schools at West Chester are included with those having had high school work.

Many of the Seniors had had no previous high school work, the percentage of those without any varying from 20.4 at Millersville to 55.2 at Shippensburg, with both the average and the central tendency[1] at 39.5 per cent. Upon the other hand, comparatively few of the Seniors had had a full four-year high school course. Kutztown makes the poorest showing with but 7 per cent and Indiana the best with 25.9 per cent. The central tendency for the eleven normal schools is 14.9 per cent and the average is 16.5 per cent for those having completed work in a regular secondary school.

Seniors also have an abnormal number of daily recitations requiring definite preparation. Kutztown is the only one of the eleven schools in which more than 50 per cent of the Seniors have as few as five recitations per day requiring definite preparation; in a majority of the schools less than a third of the students have as few. In fact in most, over 50 per cent of the Seniors have from six to eight recitations, and over 30 per cent have seven or more. The situation seems even more impossible when consideration is given to the fact that during the year 1909-1910 observation and practice teaching were required in the model school, and the students were expected to make out lesson plans and to apply the principles presented in the professional courses.

In the following table, Table 5, two comparisons are made. One is between the students in the three-year course of the Pennsylvania state normals, and the students in the two-year course of six outside state normals; the former have no definite entrance requirements, while the latter insist upon high school graduation or its equivalent. The other comparison is between the students of the Pennsylvania three-year course and those of two Illinois normal schools, which have a four-year course for common school graduates, but which offer a special two-year course to students from recognized high schools. Below is the table making these comparisons:

---

[1] The central tendency is used in place of the technical word *median*, which is defined as the measure above which and below which are an equal number of cases. It is always a safer measure than the average.

TABLE 5.—Contrasting the student body in the Pennsylvania normal schools with those in several outside state normals as to the amount of previous high school work.

Name of School	Total number reporting	Percentage having had 1 year of high school work	Percentage having had 2 years of high school work	Percentage having had 3 years of high school work	Percentage having had 4 years of high school work	Percentage from private schools	Percentage having had from 1 to 4 years of high school work	Percentage having had no high school work
Fitchburg, Mass..	161	0	0	0	100.0	*	100.0	0
Hyannis, Mass...	35	0	0	17.1	80.0	*	97.1	2.9
Salem, Mass.....	172	0	0	0	100.0	*	100.0	0
Worcester, Mass..	105	1.0	0	0	99.0	*	100.0	0
Montclair, N. J...	319	0	0	0	100.0	*	100.0	0
San Jose, Cal....	509	0.2	0.8	3.7	94.1	*	98.8	1.2
Total.......	1301	0.2	0.3	1.9	97.1	*	99.5	0.5
Pennsylvania† ...	3572	9.2	15.3	17.6	11.9	2.0	56.0	44.0
Normal, Ill......	393	12.2	12.7	13.0	31.8	*	69.7	30.3
Charleston, Ill...	325	3.1	7.7	9.2	27.7	0	47.7	52.3

* Number from private schools are included with those having had high school work.
† This includes the Junior and Middle-year students in ten of the thirteen normal schools, and the Seniors in eleven.

The first comparison shows two or three startling differences. In the six outside normals, giving a two-year course based upon graduation from high schools of good standing, 97.1 per cent of the students have had four years of high school work, while but 11.9 per cent of the 3572 Pennsylvania students have had the same. A pupil graduating from any one of the six outside normal schools would be compelled to complete four years of academic and two of professional study above the common schools; a student in a Pennsylvania normal seldom spends more than three years, certainly not more than four, of academic and professional study above the work of the common schools.

Though the students in the Pennsylvania normals are not in any sense the academic equals of the students in the six outside normal schools, yet they carry many more studies requiring definite preparation. With the exception of the Worcester, Massachusetts, normal, none of the outside normal students carry more than five studies, while 37.8 per cent of the Pennsylvania students carry six studies; 24.8 per cent carry seven, and over ten per cent pretend to carry eight or nine daily subjects requiring definite preparation In a word, the Pennsylvania students with poor preparation attempt to do more than do students with much better preparation. This condition must necessarily affect the efficiency of these Pennsylvania students when they become public school teachers.

The second comparison is also not in favor of the Pennsylvania normal schools, though at first glance this might be the inference. For instance, 44 per cent of the 3572 Pennsylvania students have had no high school work, as against 52.3 per cent for Charleston. When it is recalled that practically all the Pennsylvania students who enter directly from the common schools are graduated in three years, instead of four as at Charleston, the comparison takes a different aspect. When it is further recalled that many of the Pennsylvania students are allowed to shorten the time by combining the work of two years in one, while at Charleston no such opportunity is given and every student from the common schools must have four years of work, the comparison is undoubtedly in favor of Charleston. It may be added here that in Illinois no student is allowed to shorten the time of study. A high school graduate must take two full years, a graduate from a non-accredited high school must take three full years, and a graduate from the common schools must take four full years. This, as has been previously stated, is not the case in Pennsylvania since many students can be graduated in less than the stipulated time. For instance, at East Stroudsburg in 1909, 25 students from four-year high schools were graduated in one year and like instances can be cited from other Pennsylvania schools.

Again the Pennsylvania normals suffer when comparison is made between them and the two Illinois normals with respect to the number of daily recitations requiring definite preparation. For instance, 59.5 per cent of the students at Normal, Illinois, and 81.2 per cent at Charleston, Illinois, have but four recitations, while as few as 3.6 per cent of the Pennsylvania students have the same number. In Pennsylvania, 22.1 per cent have five recitations as against 17.4 for the Illinois schools. Practically none of the Illinois students are permitted to carry more than five studies, but in Pennsylvania, where the students try to do in three years what the Illinois students find difficult to do in four years, 37.8 per cent have six and 24.8 per cent have seven daily recitations requiring definite preparation. In fact, 74.2 per cent have 6 or over against 2.91 per cent for both the Illinois schools. The figures would be still higher if a complete record of those students attempting to do two years' work in one could have been obtained.

In most of the Pennsylvania normal schools the classes are very large. This is true of even the most prosperous schools. Less regard seems to be given to the size of the classes in the professional subjects than to any other. Even at West Chester, where the financial conditions are excellent, five of the sections in Methods and School Management during the year 1909-1910 enrolled from 78 to 83; at Bloomsburg the classes in the three professional studies enrolled from 50 to 60. At Clarion the number ran from 75 to 128; at Edinboro from 70 to 120; at Indiana from 50 to 54; at Lock Haven from 112 to 150; and at Mansfield and Slippery Rock from 80 to 93.

The classes in the academic subjects were also abnormally large. At Edinboro the three sections in botany, which requires laboratory work, had an enrollment in each from 50 to 60 students; 20 of the classes in academic subjects in Indiana ranged in size from 30 to 50, and the classes at Kutztown were equally large. At Mansfield both the Virgil and Caesar classes enrolled 45 students. Probably the conditions were even worse at Lock Haven, Millersville, and Slippery Rock. At Lock Haven a dozen classes enrolled from 35 in Caesar to 60 in trigonometry, German, botany and physics. At Millersville one laboratory section in zoölogy had 58 students and another in botany had 60, while nine other classes had an enrollment from 40 to 71 students. The condition at Slippery Rock was even worse: one Latin section had 67 students, and the Junior algebra class had over 80; the two senior sections in English had respectively 85 and 90, while the botany and zoölogy sections each had from 75 to 90.

Probably in no first-class high school in the country can a

like condition be found. In the Butler high school, located within a few miles of Slippery Rock, the laboratory work is much more efficiently conducted than in most of the Pennsylvania normal schools, and the classes are of reasonable size. No high school principal would think of having a class of 50 or 60 in Latin or German. At the Erie high school, not far from Edinboro, the laboratory equipment is far superior to that found in the normal school, and no class during the past year had an enrollment above 30 pupils.

The above discussion has been confined to the regular classes in the Pennsylvania normal schools; but a study of the student body in these institutions would not be complete without an examination of the preparatory or Sub-Junior class which is to be found in practically every one of the thirteen Pennsylvania normals.

The following table, Table 6, gives facts concerning over five hundred Sub-Juniors enrolled in seven of the Pennsylvania normal schools:

TABLE 6.—Giving facts concerning the Sub-Juniors in the Pennsylvania normal schools for 1909–1910 as to the amount of previous high school work and the number of daily recitations requiring definite preparation.

Name of School	Total number reporting	Percentage having had 1 year of high school work	Percentage having had 2 years of high school work	Percentage having had 3 years of high school work	Percentage having had 4 years of high school work	Percentage from private schools	Percentage having had from 1 to 4 years of high school work	Percentage having had no high school work
Clarion	69	13.0	13.0	7.3	0	0	33.3	66.7
Indiana	63	9.5	7.9	1.6	0	0	6.4	25.4	74.6
Kutztown	41	2.4	2.4	0	0	2.4	7.2	92.8
Lock Haven	15	0	0	0	0	0	0	100.0
Millersville	151	12.6	11.9	6.0	3.3	0.7	34.5	65.5
Slippery Rock	46	6.5	6.5	4.4	0	2.2	19.6	80.4
West Chester	173	2.3	13.9	14.4	8.7	5.8	45.1	54.9
Total	558	7.5	10.8	7.5	3.6	3.0	32.4	67.6

A careful study of Table 6 shows that 67.6 per cent of the sub-juniors have had no high school work whatever, and only 11.1 have had three or four years at a secondary school. Most of the students who had previously attended high school had not been graduated. Pupils in this lowest class of the normal schools also had an impossible number of recitations: 37.3 per cent had six recitations; 22.0 per cent seven, and 13.1 per cent tried to carry eight or nine daily recitations requiring definite preparation.

One hundred and fifty or 27.95 per cent of the 558 sub-juniors had had some teaching experience. Eighty-two or 14.9 per cent had taught one year, and 34 or 6.18 per cent had taught two years. The normal school authorities may claim that a distinct service is rendered the state by caring for these inefficient teachers and adding somewhat to their skill and effectiveness. This might be granted if it were not for the fact that in this same normal class are another group that have no place in a professional school, since they belong to the upper grades of a common school or the first year of a high school. At the end of one year or even in less time some of these pupils use the name of the normal in order to obtain a license and a school, though in no sense of the word are they prepared to teach. The establishment of a Sub-Junior class by Kutztown, Millersville, Slippery Rock, West Chester and other Pennsylvania normals undoubtedly tends to lower the professional standards in the immediate neighborhood of the schools, since most of the sub-juniors come from the local normal school counties.

To sum up, this Sub-Junior class is composed of many boys and girls from the sixth, seventh, and eighth grades; of older students who found it hard to do satisfactory work in a high school in their own neighborhood, and of teachers of two or three years' experience who have much difficulty to obtain a provisional certificate and who seldom aspire to continue the normal course and fit themselves properly for their work.

This class is merely preparatory and has no place in the normal, but it is kept in most schools for two definite reasons: in the first place, principals are thus assured of a goodly number of juniors for the following year, and in the second place, for those that are 17 years or over the schools receive $1.50 a week from the state simply by enrolling them in a Methods Course.

Although the defects of the Pennsylvania normals are mainly due to the fact that these institutions are under private lay control, the normal school law[1] is nevertheless to a considerable extent responsible for some of the shortcomings of these institutions. Especially does it affect the student body, for because of the manner of distributing " state aid," a premium is placed upon gross numbers and therefore the principal must see to it that a large student body is enrolled. The result is that instead of raising the teaching profession to a level with the other professions, thereby enabling it to fulfill its obligations to society, these institutions actually retard the educational advancement of some localities because, to have successful schools, the principals are obliged to lower the standards, admit all applicants, and finally to send forth into the teaching profession many young men and women poorly equipped for their important duties.

---

[1] The new school law of 1911 does not correct this evil.

CHAPTER IX

THE FACULTY

With few exceptions, the faculties of the Pennsylvania normal schools are composed of fine-spirited, earnest men and women who have the best interests of their pupils at heart and who give their whole energy to their school. In the main, these teachers are both overworked and underpaid, and because of this, certain unfortunate conditions have come about which deserve full description and consideration. As in previous chapters, it will be shown that private control of these publicly-supported institutions has either created or accentuated these adverse conditions.

In order to analyze in detail the status of teaching in these institutions, a complete history of 265 of the instructors has been obtained. Of these, slightly more than half have attended some normal school, often the one in which they are now teaching. It was found that 183 of the 265 have had from one to four years of college training, and 117 hold the bachelor's degree.

A large number of the Pennsylvania colleges which many of the normal school teachers attended, however, are very small and lead a precarious existence; and many of them, probably 40 per cent, give work not more than one or two years above a good high school course.

This naturally leads to the question of the value of degrees, both earned and honorary. In each instance the highest degree of the individual has been taken as the most representative. Of the 47 A. M. degrees reported, 27 or 57.4 per cent were earned. Of the 22 doctor's degrees reported, 45.4 per cent were earned. Six of these degrees as well as six of the master's were conferred by such institutions as Kansas City University, Washington and Jefferson College, and Worcester University for work done in absence.

The higher educational institutions of Pennsylvania and other

74

states have conferred, all told, seventy-seven honorary degrees upon the teachers in these thirteen state normal schools. At Bloomsburg five of the teachers have received the honorary A. B. and six the honorary A. M. degree. Most of these titles have been conferred by Lafayette College. It is surprising to learn that thirty-six honorary A. M. degrees have been given, but it is still more surprising to find that eleven men have received the honorary title of Doctor of Philosophy. These titles have been conferred by Lafayette, Wittenberg, Bucknell, Washington and Jefferson, and Wesleyan University (Ohio), and one or two other institutions. Bucknell College has also given the honorary Doctor of Science degree to two teachers.

A study has been made of the teaching experience of the members of the normal school faculties before they accepted their present positions. Thirty, or 11.4 per cent of the 265 reporting the amount of previous experience, had never taught before. Only 226 state specifically the kind of position they had previously held. Eight had been city superintendents, and a majority of these eight have since become normal school principals; nineteen had been high school or ward principals; twenty-six had been engaged in teaching in some of the smaller Pennsylvania colleges; one hundred and fifty-six had been only common- or graded-school teachers: and but 17, or 7.5 per cent, had had previous normal school experience. Most of these 17 had been employed in other Pennsylvania normal schools, which indicates that it has been the policy of a majority of the principals never to go outside the state to supply vacancies. As a consequence, the Pennsylvania normal schools have too seldom been able to compare their methods and results with those of other state normal schools. This is made still more evident, when it is considered that as many as 156, or 69 per cent, of the 226 had taught only in the grades or common schools.

These figures undoubtedly indicate that the normal schools are willing to take persons with no experience whatever, or persons who have simply become skilled in teaching the common school branches, rather than to engage individuals who have specialized in a particular subject at a first-rate college, university, or school of education. There are exceptions, but this undoubtedly is the tendency. One exception to this is found at the

Indiana normal where a large group of graduates from the best colleges in the east and the middle-west has recently been added to the faculty.

A tabulation of the native residence of 289 of the normal school teachers shows that 84 of these persons, or 29 per cent, were reared in the thirteen counties where these schools are situated. A more significant fact is that 201, or 69.5 per cent of the 289 teachers whose residences were obtained, claim Pennsylvania as their native residence.

It is reasonable to assume that a very large proportion of men should come from within the state itself; it is most desirable that this should be so; but it is unfortunate that not more often a leading educator from an adjoining state has been chosen, since few of the principals or other leading normal men have availed themselves of any opportunity to go abroad and compare their system of schools with those of other countries.

One notable exception, and only one can be cited to this sweeping assertion, and that is the case of the former principal of the California state normal, the late Doctor Theodore B. Noss, who had enough faith in himself and his work to go abroad for two years to discover first-hand what other countries were doing to make the teaching profession stronger and more serviceable. The loss of this man to the educational interests of the state of Pennsylvania is severe.

A study of the salaries shows that the average pay for the 284 teachers is $1,274.40, with 223 below and 61 above the average, and with the central tendency at $961.[1] One hundred and fifty-five teachers receive between $700 and $1,100 inclusive. An investigation of the comparative salaries of the men and women teachers shows that the former are much better paid. The average salary paid the 137 women is $782.88,[2] and the average paid the 134 men (the thirteen principals being excluded) is $1,176.67. These averages are very close to the central tendency since 65 women have higher and 72 lower salaries than their average indicates, and 77 of the 137 women receive

[1] The central tendency is used in place of the technical work *median*, which is defined as the measure above which and below which are an equal number of cases.

[2] Two hundred dollars has been added to the salary of each teacher living free of charge in the school dormitory for ten months of the year. Often, however, this teacher is compelled to do extra work in the way of hall duty and disciplining to pay for this increase in salary.

salaries ranging from $700 to $900 inclusive; and 64 men have higher and 70 have lower salaries than their average given above, and 73 of the 134 men receive salaries ranging from $1,000 to $1,400 inclusive. Only 23 women receive $1,000 or over, and but one woman has a salary of above $1,200. Her salary, which is $1,400, is equaled or surpassed by 38, or over one-fourth, of the entire number of men teachers.

The amount of service required for these ordinary salaries is considerable. Practically all the normal teachers in the state institutions have six recitations per day or thirty per week; in but one of the thirteen schools, California, is there a tendency to keep the number down to five a day or twenty-five a week. One normal school principal believes that thirty a week is not excessive.

To add very much to the labor of the teachers, many of the classes are extremely large. Probably no high school in the state has such enormous classes. Since the details as to the size of classes have been given in the chapter on the normal school students, the subject is considered here only as it adds to the burden of the teachers.

Undoubtedly these instructors can do little in the way of self-improvement during the regular school term. Under the circumstances it is surprising that they are able to keep well since besides the regular teaching many of them are expected and practically compelled to aid in the social life of the school. A number of the men look after the coaching and management of athletic teams, while the women are called upon to assist the girls in their social activities. Because of the dormitory life in all these institutions, the extra demands upon the teachers are many and heavy.

Since it is practically impossible for these teachers to improve their scholarship under these adverse conditions, it is important to discover how many have been able or willing to obtain leave of absence from their work for such a purpose. Of all the teachers whose records have been obtained, only five or six have had a full year's leave of absence since beginning work in their present position. The case of the late Doctor Noss, of the California normal, who went abroad for two years, has already been cited as a distinct exception. Only 90 of the

Pennsylvania normal school teachers have done any advanced work since taking their present position and forty-eight of these, or 53 per cent of the 90, have had work for but one or two summers in some of the eastern universities or at a Chautauqua; very few of the others have gone abroad for even two or three months; while five or six others have taken special work in some nearby higher educational institution for a semester at week-ends.

Since 156, or more than 50 per cent of these teachers have not had anything more than graded-school or common-school experience, we can understand what the present situation means. Because of the large classes, skill in schoolroom management is very important, and this is assured by getting practical teachers from the field. Scholarship is not in considerable demand in any one of the institutions. If a man or woman of true scholarship is employed, his zeal for research and his desire for growth are soon lost in the treadmill of six or seven recitations per day and in the additional duties that are required in the dormitories, the athletic activities, and in the social life.

Here again are to be found other evils largely due to the domination by private lay boards. In accordance with the interpretation of the laws by the state superintendent, the selection and remuneration of teachers lie wholly in the hands of the trustees. Many of these boards are composed of men who have very limited incomes and naturally do not look with favor upon a proposition to give " school teachers " what they consider enormous salaries. Even men of large incomes cannot understand how school teachers can expect to receive reasonable compensation. When suit was brought against officials of the West Chester normal to prevent them from taking from the normal school treasury between $25,000 and $26,000, they replied by criticizing the school expenditures, and they especially objected to the " high salaries " paid the instructors. The officials of all the Pennsylvania normal schools have gone out into the open market to secure teachers for the smallest amount of money. Their refusal to pay reasonable salaries has resulted in the following adverse conditions:

1. Often they obtain in the local normal school district rather efficient teachers who in order to remain near home are willing

to work for a lower salary than they would accept elsewhere, but who are not financially able to continue their studies in higher institutions. This accounts for much of the inbreeding.

2. Occasionally they employ teachers from outside the state who through lack of initiative, or perhaps ambition, or by accident, accept positions in these schools. Some of them are content to remain in spite of the low salaries.

It may be added that a number of the Pennsylvania teachers can bear comparison with the best in other states; but many cannot, and the longer they remain in these institutions the greater will be the contrast since low salaries, an abnormal number of recitations per day, lack of reward for graduate study and high scholarship, and additional burdens due to the dormitory life of the schools have prevented the best teachers in these institutions from reaching their highest efficiency and have enabled the poorly equipped and inefficient to continue for a long time in their present positions.

It is a simple economic question: if the state normal schools in Massachusetts, New Jersey, Illinois, New York, and practically all the other northern and western states pay better salaries, they will eventually attract the best men and women in Pennsylvania and only those of second-rate ability will remain. Pennsylvania must enter into competition with these states or her educational interests will continue to suffer.

CHAPTER X

THE RELATION OF THE STATE NORMAL SCHOOLS TO THE PUBLIC HIGH SCHOOLS

The Pennsylvania State normal schools and the public high schools are to-day in direct conflict. In previous chapters it has been shown that a large number of the normal school students belong to the high school period, and their academic preparation is such that they should be attending the secondary schools in their own neighborhood. In the past it was undoubtedly true that the high schools of the state were so few and so inadequate that it was absolutely necessary for the state normal schools to give academic work of secondary grade. For the last ten years, however, there has been increasingly less need for the normal schools to devote time and energy to academic instruction, but strange to say the normal school principals as late as 1910 agreed upon a four-year course of study that possesses many characteristics of the ordinary high school and places their institutions in direct competition with the rapidly increasing public high schools.

The increasing demand for well-equipped teachers caused the early educational leaders of Pennsylvania to look about for some type of institution that would meet the needs of the public school system. The plan of leaving the preparation of teachers wholly to private initiative had failed; the plan to subsidize church and private academies and colleges had likewise failed. The efforts of the educators finally resulted in the normal school act of 1857, which promised no financial assistance, but set a standard of work for one institution in each of the twelve (later thirteen) districts. Graduates of these schools were to receive permanent teachers' certificates.

Many of these normal schools were established on the ruins of old academies which had suspended operation or were on the verge of closing their doors. Because of the fact that these old academies had done high school work, and because of the need in

80

certain communities for such grade of work, these new institutions became and have remained in many respects more like academies of the old type than what they pretended to be,— professional schools. At the beginning the lack of high schools was not due so much to the existence of the state normals as to the independence of each school district and the failure of the leading school men of Pennsylvania to induce the legislature to pass laws encouraging the establishment of secondary schools. Occasionally, cities like Philadelphia or Harrisburg would ask the legislature for permission to erect a high school. But the state of Pennsylvania had few first-class high schools as late as 1890, and the following year, Doctor D. J. Waller, Jr., then state superintendent, in his annual report commented at length on the great lack of high schools and the need for proper legislation.

The first general law authorizing the establishment of public high schools was passed in 1895, long after many eastern and middle western states had completed the establishment of a system of secondary schools which enabled the children of any community to continue their education in preparation for college, for business, or for a profession.

This law as State Superintendent Schaeffer has explained, " divides high schools into three classes, specifies the basis upon which money appropriated in aid of high schools shall be distributed, and prescribes the scholarship of at least one of the teachers to be employed in a high school receiving State aid." The law defines a first grade high school as one " maintaining four years of study beyond the branches of learning prescribed to be taught in the common schools;" a second grade as one maintaining three years; and a third grade as one maintaining two years. High schools of the first grade were to receive $800, those of the second $600, and those of the third, $400. It was also stipulated that no high school could receive state aid unless one teacher is " legally certified to teach bookkeeping, civics, general history, algebra, geometry, trigonometry, including plane surveying, rhetoric, English literature, Latin, including Caesar, Virgil and Cicero, and the elements of physics, chemistry, including the chemistry of soils, botany, geology and zoölogy, including entomology, and no teacher shall be employed to teach any branch or branches of learning other than those enumerated in his or her certificate."[1] This requirement is of great advantage to the state normal schools, and proves that these institutions have been a factor in restricting, or at least determining all the high school legislation. 'This requirement will be discussed later in some detail.

The first state aid for secondary education was given in 1901 when the legislature appropriated $50,000 for township high schools. In some respects this appropriation was injurious because practically no standards were laid down. Since no provision was made for high school inspection, the State Superintendent of Public Instruction was compelled to distribute money to many schools that in no real sense met these few standards. As a consequence many "advanced grammar schools" were called high schools and received state aid. Since that time, the public school officials of Pennsylvania have had to devote much time and energy to the reconstruction of these so-called high schools.

The greatest good accomplished by this first appropriation was in committing the state of Pennsylvania to a policy which has proved of immense value to Massachusetts, New York, Minnesota, and other progressive states. Some time in the future the wealthy state of Pennsylvania may provide for "the pupils of the country districts school advantages equal to those within reach of boys and girls in the cities."

Later, the state legislature was induced to extend its appropriations and include borough high schools; but it was not until 1907 that it gave $12,000, more by accident than by design, for high school inspection which should naturally have been provided for when the first money was appropriated. As a consequence, thousands of dollars of the state's money have been wasted and many communities have been taught to accept poor for excellent high school facilities for their children. The first year high school inspectors were employed, they refused state aid to over seventy schools, thereby saving between $25,000 and $30,000 to the state. At the same time, they prevented the establishment of new high schools that could not offer proper educational facilities to boys and girls.

It was asserted at the beginning of this chapter that the

---

[1] The essential features of this classification remain in the Act. of 1911.

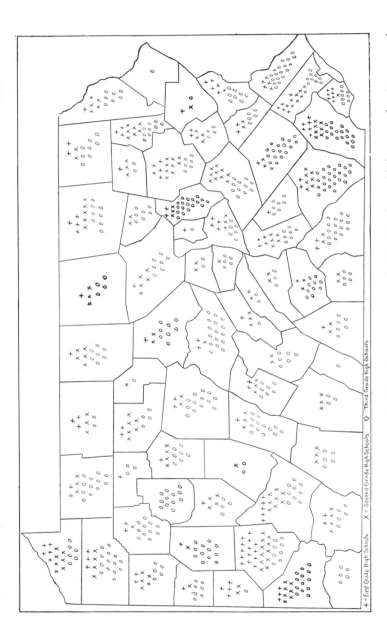

A chart showing the influence of the Pennsylvania state normal schools in the establishment and maintenance of first grade (four year,) second grade (three year,) and third grade (two year) high schools. The normal schools are situated in the counties containing the red characters.

The sixty-six counties (exclusive of Philadelphia) have four hundred and ninety-three third grade high schools, while the thirteen normal school counties alone contain one hundred and forty-five of these two-year high schools. Proportionally, these thirteen counties should contain less than one hundred such schools.

The figures quoted above were obtained from the report of the Pennsylvania high school inspectors for the year 1908-1909.

+ = First Grade High Schools   X = Second Grade High Schools   O = Third Grade High Schools

Pennsylvania state normal schools are to-day in opposition to the growth and efficiency of the high schools. A study of the distribution of the three grades of high schools in the state bears out the assertion that the conflict is disastrous to the better secondary schools.

Most of the normals are surrounded by high schools of the third grade. At Millersville, one of the largest incorporated villages in the state, which has a population of 1,600, there is no high school except that belonging to the model school at the state normal. This high school, established in 1906, maintains but a three-year course. Most of the teaching is done by eighteen practice teachers, who are seniors in the normal. The total enrollment is but forty-five. In a like town in the middle-west, the enrollment would be over one hundred. At Slippery Rock, the high school is part of the model school and is a feeder for the local state normal.

At East Stroudsburg, with a population of about 3,500, the local high school has a three-year course and an enrollment of but fifty-seven. The attendance should be between one hundred and fifty and two hundred. The main business of this school is to prepare students for the normal. The names of the classes have been changed to conform to those of the normal grades,— Junior, Middle, Senior. This high school has poor library and laboratory facilities.

The little town of Mansfield has been content to maintain a poor high school. The pupils have three years' work above that of the grades, and devote much time to the study of arithmetic, English grammar, and American history so that they may be admitted to the middle-year at the local state normal. At Shippensburg, a city of 3,500, the total high school enrollment is ninety-five. Two of the three teachers employed are simply normal graduates; in fact it is the policy of the Shippensburg board of education to select normal graduates as teachers. The laboratory equipment in this school is worth less than two hundred dollars.

At Edinboro, a town of 1,000 inhabitants in a good agricultural district, the three-year high school enrolls sixty pupils. The supervising principal, a college graduate, teaches nine classes each day, and his assistant, a graduate of the local normal, has

ten classes. The high school has no laboratory facilities. Many who would otherwise attend this high school have been enrolled as students in the local state normal.

Kutztown has a third grade school with but one teacher and with an enrollment of fourteen, though the school district has a population of three thousand. The normal enrolls many of the students who should be attending the local high school. At Indiana, a city of 7,000 inhabitants, the high school, which should have over three hundred students, last year enrolled but one hundred and thirty-seven. The laboratory equipment is probably worth one hundred dollars. This school has been rated by the high school inspectors as third grade.[1] At Clarion, a city of 3,000 or over, the two-year high school has an enrollment of thirty-six and but one regular teacher.

In practically all the normal school towns, the only way of reaching a first class college or professional school is by attending the local state normal, or by going to a first grade high school away from home and frequently outside the county.

This state of affairs is both undemocratic and wasteful. If the thousands of dollars given to the state normals of Pennsylvania for purely high school teaching were devoted to the establishment and support of public high schools under adequate and wise supervision, the result would be both startling and salutary. In the end it would enable the normal schools to become strictly professional, and it would encourage the establishment of an adequate system of secondary schools which would raise considerably the educational standards for the entire state.

The condition of secondary education in Pennsylvania even outside the normal school environment is far from satisfactory. In order to understand the status of the secondary schools, blanks asking for detailed information were sent to representative high schools of each grade, in every county in the state, and replies were received from a majority. In addition, high schools in various parts of the commonwealth were personally inspected and many public school men were consulted.

The facts thus obtained reveal several striking defects. They show that even many of the first grade high schools have meagre laboratory equipment, and little money has been spent recently

---

[1] The state high school inspectors in 1910-1911 rated the Indiana high school as second grade.

by the school directors to rectify this defect. The first and second grade schools have spent more money for physics than for all the other sciences combined. Less than half as much has been used for chemistry, while the laboratory facilities for botany, zoölogy, and physical geography are practically worthless. The average total expenditure for laboratory equipment for the first grade high schools is $1,069.60 and for the second grade but $280.40, while the central tendency for the first is $750 and for the second $200. Practically none of the third grade high schools have any laboratory. Few of the schools of even the first grade have good working libraries and reference books.

The teachers in these high schools have too many recitations: the average for those in the first grade is 6.5, with the central tendency at 6.93 per day; for those in the second, the average is 7.87, with the central tendency at 8.25; and for those in the third grade the average is 8.48, and the central tendency 7.88, with 44 per cent teaching from ten to thirteen daily recitations.

The salaries of the Pennsylvania high school teachers are too low. In the schools of the first grade reporting, the central tendency in salary is $84.06; for the second grade, it is $77.50, and for the third grade, $70.63. The central tendency in salary for all the teachers is $80.10. These salaries, running from seven to nine months, are so meagre that the best teachers soon find positions in the large city high schools or leave the profession altogether, and the tendency is for only those of mediocre ability to be retained for any length of time.

The attendance in all grades, as shown by the facts obtained, is very small. For all these schools, the average attendance is 83 pupils with the central tendency at 58.75 per school. At the same time, the average population for a school district was found to be 5,318 with the central tendency at 3,087. This indicates conclusively that comparatively few boys and girls in Pennsylvania are attending high schools.

In quality, size and number, the Pennsylvania high schools are in contrast to those of many other states, due largely to the fact that the state has not aided and directed them properly. In 1902 when " sixty-six Pennsylvania town-ship high schools came up to the legal standard and received their share of aid," the first ever given by that state, Ohio, with much less wealth and with over two million less population, had six hundred and ninety-nine township high schools. This contrast was discussed by State Superintendent Schaeffer, of Pennsylvania, in his annual report for that year. A few years ago, New Jersey gave to her state board of education the authority to supervise all public high schools. At present it gives from three to four hundred dollars for every teacher employed in secondary schools maintaining a definite standard. In fact for the past ten years most of the northern and western states have given annually many thousands of dollars for the betterment of their system of secondary schools. Moreover, they have taken care to have this money wisely and legitimately expended.

The following table, Table 7, made from statistics given in the annual report of the United States Commissioner of Education for 1908-1909, compares Pennsylvania with six other states as to population, wealth, total number of secondary schools with their enrollment and teachers, and proportion of secondary pupils to the entire population:

TABLE 7.—Comparing Pennsylvania with six other states as to population, wealth, number of high schools, number of teachers and pupils in these schools and relative number of high school pupils to the population.*

Name of State	No. of schools	No. of teachers	No. of students	Popula-tion	Total assessed valuation	No. of students to every 1,000 popu-lation
Pennsylvania .	731	2520	59,183	6,302,115	$5,769,777,327	9
New York....	596	4041	101,497	7,268,894	9,666,118,681	14
Massachusetts	223	1983	51,823	2,805,346	4,574,136,145	18
Ohio.........	812	2638	60,280	4,157,545	2,352,680,824	15
Indiana......	629	1955	42,322	2,516,462	1,776,132,096	17
Illinois.......	565	2500	58,991	4,821,550	1,263,500,487	12
Minnesota....	199	1086	23,613	1,751,394	1,090,684,936	14

* Statistics as to schools, teachers, and pupils, were taken from the report for 1908–1909 of the United States Commissioner of Education. Statistics as to population and wealth were obtained from the World's Almanac.

A casual glance at this table shows an advantage for Pennsylvania since during the year 1908-1909, that state claimed to have 731 high schools, which is in excess of the number in any of the others except Ohio. But an analysis of the table shows that this superiority is apparent, not real: a large number of these Pennsylvania high schools are such in name only. For this same year, the Pennsylvania state high school inspectors reported that over 490 of these secondary schools belonged to the third grade,—a two-year course, with one or two teachers, and practically no library or laboratory equipment.

The table shows that Pennsylvania with 18 per cent more schools has 38 per cent less teachers than the state of New York; and though it has 69 per cent more high schools than Massachusetts, it has only 21 per cent more teachers. Such differences are not to be explained by the congested condition of Massachusetts and New York; distinctly agricultural states like Ohio and Indiana make as good a showing as Pennsylvania, while Illinois and Minnesota with more territory and considerably smaller population provide superior advantages in the way of better equipped schools.

The last column of the above table tells its own story: a fair proportion of the boys and girls of Pennsylvania are not enrolled in the secondary schools. The condition in Pennsylvania is much worse than it is in Massachusetts, which has added a very large foreign population to its citizenship within the past fifteen years. Minnesota has also a large foreign population, probably as difficult to assimilate as the foreigners that have been attracted to many districts in Pennsylvania. Yet Minnesota through state aid and wise state supervision has carefully distributed her first class high schools in an area nearly twice as large as that of Pennsylvania, and among a population less than a fifth as numerous so that equal opportunities could be afforded the country boys and girls and the children of foreign-born parents who are unable to pay tuition in private acadamies. As a consequence, out of every one thousand persons in Minnesota, 14 attend public high schools, which is 36 per cent greater than the number attending similar institutions in Pennsylvania. Massachusetts makes even a better showing, since it exceeds Pennsylvania by 50 per cent; but even agricultural states like Ohio, Indiana, and Illinois, with a much smaller population and much less wealth, are able to put Pennsylvania to shame.

An analysis of other figures given by the Commissioner of Education shows the following interesting facts as to the per-

88

Pennsylvania State Normal Schools

centage of high schools having a full four-year course in each of these states:

[1] In Pennsylvania   34.4 per cent have a four-year course.
In New York   83.0 per cent have a four-year course.
In Massachusetts   90.5 per cent have a four-year course.
In Ohio   55.7 per cent have a four-year course.
In Indiana   66.9 per cent have a four-year course.
In Illinois   68.7 per cent have a four-year course.
In Minnesota   98.9 per cent have a four-year course.

This comparison shows that Pennsylvania stands last among the seven states in spite of her large population and great wealth, which morally obligate her to establish and maintain a complete system of well-equipped first grade high schools.

What is the safest and most desirable avenue leading out of this chaos? Under what condition can Pennsylvania have an efficient system of secondary schools?

1. The section of the high school law of 1895[2] relating to the certification of high school teachers should be changed. At present it is required by this law that each school receiving state aid shall have at least one teacher legally certified to teach practically all the secondary schools subjects. By accident or design, these are the identical subjects found to-day in the normal school curriculum, and therefore, a normal diploma is a license to teach in any high school of the state. It is difficult for a college graduate to comply with this law, especially if he has been sensible enough to concentrate his time and energy upon a specialty. The law tends to place in the high schools of the state many normal graduates who are not qualified since their academic work in the normal school is purely secondary in character.

2. The third grade high schools should be combined into

---

[1] In the report of the Pennsylvania state high school inspectors for 1908-1909, only 96 four-year high schools were rated as first-grade. If this fact is considered, then Pennsylvania drops to 17 per cent. This report of the inspectors excludes a very few city high schools which receive no state aid.

[2] The law of 1911, though much like the law of 1895, is an improvement. It provides that "a sufficient number of the teachers" shall be employed to teach any of the following branches: "bookkeeping, civil government, general history, algebra, geometry, rhetoric, English Literature, Latin (including Caesar, Virgil, and Cicero) physical geography, and the elements of botany, of zoölogy, of physics, and of chemistry. But no teacher shall be employed to teach any branch other than those enumerated in his certificate."

fewer joint high schools with a full four-year course, with well-prepared teachers, and good laboratory and library facilities.[1]

3. Districts not containing a first grade high school should be required to pay the tuition of all pupils who desire to attend such a school outside these districts.[2] It should be added that one hundred thousand dollars has already been granted by the Pennsylvania legislature for this purpose. The public school system of every district and of every county should be such as to lead by direct steps from the country and graded school to the local high school, and from the local high school to the best colleges, universities, technical and professional schools of the country. Otherwise the children of parents of limited means have no opportunity to compete with the children of the wealthy. A democracy means equal opportunity, and this cannot come to the thousands of Pennsylvania children until they have opened to them a system of secondary education as good as that found in Massachusetts, New York, Ohio, Indiana, Minnesota, and many other states.

4. In the near future, Pennsylvania should have two or three additional high school inspectors with increased authority. The state must also provide more money to the first grade high schools. To make the secondary system of schools still more efficient, the state should also provide elementary school inspection.[3]

5. The conflict of interest between the state normal schools and the struggling public high schools should cease. The state normal schools should not be permitted to enroll a single student until he has been graduated from a first grade high school.

So long as the Pennsylvania normal schools are publicly supported and privately controlled and so long as they admit students from the common schools and the third-grade high schools, they will not be able to discharge their proper function, and they will retard the establishment and development of a splendid system of high-grade secondary schools. The state normals or private high schools of Pennsylvania receive pay for doing work which if done by high schools would be both more thorough and less expensive, and would reach thousands of children that today are sadly neglected.

Such is the condition in a state, which though surpassed by but one other of the entire forty-eight states in either population

---

[1] The new law makes provision for the establishment of such joint schools.

[2] This provision is embodied in the new law.

[3] The new school law has made provision for additional inspectors.

or wealth, gives meagre opportunities to the children of the middle classes to obtain a thorough education. The president of a state university in the middle-west has said that " the people want open paths from every corner of the state, through the schools, to the highest and best things which men can achieve. To make such paths, to make them open to the poorest and lead to the highest, is the mission of democracy." This mission is yet to be fulfilled by the Pennsylvania public school system, and the leadership of the normal school principals cannot be enlisted in the solution of these important secondary problems until the normal schools leave the field of secondary education and confine themselves to their legitimate professional work.

CHAPTER XI

CONCLUSIONS

The greatest defect of the Pennsylvania Normal School system is the present management. This weakness, bad in itself, is especially harmful because to it can be ascribed, directly or indirectly, most of the other existing evils.

The thirteen Pennsylvania state normal schools are controlled by lay boards that look upon these institutions largely as business ventures, and are primarily interested in their financial prosperity and indifferent to their educational influence. They are, moreover, ignorant of the larger educational needs of the commonwealth. In spite of the fact that the state does not own these schools, it gives annually thousands of dollars for their support and maintenance. But worst of all it does not even supervise the expenditure of the appropriations so that these institutions may do their work satisfactorily and lead in the educational progress and reforms of the state.

Up to the present time, the state has invested in the normal schools between two and three million dollars in the form of buildings, equipment, and land. This money cannot be lost or surrendered entirely to these private corporations, and it seems that the only remedy will be for the state to assume entire control by buying up at par the outstanding stock of these school corporations. This would require at most an expenditure of five hundred thousand dollars,[1] but the state would then be able to conduct these institutions for professional purposes and put a stop to their use for private gain to the great detriment of public education.

After this first important step is taken, the other reform will come more easily, since, as has already been explained in the

---

[1] The act of 1911 provided an appropriation of $200,000 for this purpose, and decreed that a similar appropriation shall be made by each succeeding session of the legislature " until all of the state normal schools which are offered on terms acceptable to the state Board of Education have been bought."

various chapters, many other defects spring largely from the fact that these publicly-supported institutions are under the control of private corporations.

The next two defects· to be discussed are the diversity in preparation of the students enrolled, and the low entrance requirements; and since these two are so closely related, they will be considered together. First of all the lay boards demand a large enrollment rather than well-prepared students; they are encouraged in this demand by the state itself through the law which though making no stipulation as to a student's previous preparation or fitness to enroll in a professional school, grants to each institution sixty dollars a year for any student seventeen years old or above who takes " Methods." The resulting intense desire for students in order to obtain " state aid " keeps the entrance requirements so low that at graduation a student would find difficulty in obtaining Freshman standing in any one of the leading universities of the country. These conditions will undoubtedly be improved as soon as the state assumes control, for then a large enrollment will not be essential, and the standards for admission can be raised at once.

A superficial and over-crowded curriculum naturally results from a wide diversity in the preparation of the entering students. In classes, often enrolling from forty to sixty pupils, are to be found graduates of first-grade high schools and boys and girls who have not satisfactorily completed the work of the common schools. The result is disastrous to all the students, for a majority are poorly prepared when they enter, and, because of an over-crowded course of study and abnormally large classes, all are poorly equipped when they are graduated. One reform leads logically to another: as soon as the state takes control and raises the entrance requirements, the regular course of study can be modified and improved, and the many special courses, offered for the purpose of increasing the enrollment, will disappear altogether.

At present the faculties of the state normal schools are both overworked and underpaid. In the main, the lay boards of control attempt to secure cheap rather than efficient service. Little encouragement is offered to real scholarship: the time and energy of the teachers are taken up with school duties of one sort or another and self-improvement during the school term is impossible. At the same time the small salaries are effective barriers to advanced work in the summer or during a year's leave of absence. The present condition is bad, but if continued, only those of very limited scholarship, initiative, and ability will remain, while the most competent will leave to accept more lucrative positions in other states, or possibly in other professions. The remedy for this condition is clear: the state must reward efficient service with reasonable salaries.

Still further evidence of the evils of lay control and lack of state supervision by educational experts is found in the conflict existing between the normal schools and other parts of the public school system. This conflict has retarded the growth of high schools of the first grade, while it has fostered high schools of the lowest grade. The normal schools must leave the secondary field or the result will continue to be disastrous to the public school system as well as costly to the state. This evil will also disappear when a premium is no longer placed upon mere numbers and when the normal schools become really professional in character.

These are, in the main, the evils that arise from the fact that the Pennsylvania normal schools are privately-controlled but publicly-supported institutions. But as this summary should include all the more prominent defects, it is necessary to consider the conduct of the state board examinations, for which the state, and not lay control, is directly at fault. The examinations were created to maintain uniform standards, but this purpose was soon lost sight of, and to-day, because of large classes, additional duties imposed upon the examiners, and somewhat to the personnel of the boards, the system has degenerated into a formal endorsement of the recommendations of the normal school faculties. The only effect these superficial examinations have is to transform the work of the schools, especially for a month or two at the end of each year, into a cramming process in preparation for the ordeal. When the state assumes control, these examinations will be abolished, and the faculties will be held directly responsible for the work of their graduates as public school teachers.

In the introduction it was stated that the Pennsylvania school system was in such condition that it was impossible to describe it accurately without extending the study one or two years, and owing to this fact it was decided to examine but one type of institution. The state normal schools were selected, first because they are fairly representative of the system in vogue in Pennsylvania to-day except that in the other types, private local control is displaced by public local control; secondly because it was believed that one of the most potent reasons for reconstructing the Pennsylvania public school system lies in the fact that these so-called state normal schools do not have reasonably high standards of scholarship and do not co-ordinate their work with that of the public high schools. As a consequence, they do not occupy their proper sphere in the educational system, and they have not accomplished the purpose of their establishment and maintenance, since their leadership has not succeeded in placing the teaching profession on a worthy plane.

These normal schools were chosen also because their mismanagement and inefficiency are undoubtedly due to the greatest defect of the Pennsylvania school system; namely, that of leaving the direction of education to local initiative and control, public or private.

This study has shown first, that reform in a state school system is futile until the state assumes control of all examinations for those desiring to enter the teaching profession; secondly, that inevitable and costly conflicts and duplication of work will continue until a unified system is established and large supervisory powers are given to educational experts appointed for the state. Since this is true, the state should immediately assume control of the normal schools and radically change them. In fact this will be the first and most important step toward a well-correlated and unified public school system in place of the antiquated and thoroughly inadequate one now in existence. This reconstruction will eventually be made through the co-operation of the leading educators and public spirited citizens. Not until then will the wealthy state of Pennsylvania be able to say she considers her schools as important to her future welfare as her factories, her mines, and her prosperous cities. Not until then will she be able to establish an open pathway leading directly from the country and village schools to the professional schools, colleges and universities, and thereby give adequate educational facilities to the children of the poor as well as the rich.